JG 26

Photographic History of the Luftwaffe's Top Guns

Donald L. Caldwell

Motorbooks International
Publishers & Wholesalers ®

First published in 1994 by Motorbooks International Publishers & Wholesalers, PO Box 2, 729 Prospect Avenue, Osceola, WI 54020 USA

Motorbooks International books are also available at discounts in bulk quantity for industrial or sales-promotional use. For details write to Special Sales Manager at the Publisher's address

Library of Congress Cataloging-in-Publication Data
Caldwell, Donald L.
  JG 26: photographic history of the Luftwaffe's top guns/ Donald L. Caldwell.
    p. cm.
  Includes bibliographical references and index.
  ISBN 0-87938-845-5
  1. Germany. Luftwaffe. Jagdgeschwader 26 "Schlageter"—Pictorial works. 2. World War, 1939-1945—Aerial operations, German—Pictorial works. I. Title.
D787.C34   1994
940.54'4943—dc20   93-34449

On the front cover: An FW 190D-13/R11 of JG 26 painted by Jerry Crandall. Fine prints of this and other Jerry Crandall paintings are available from Eagle Editions Ltd., P.O. Box 1830, Sedona, AZ, 86336, USA. Painting copyright Eagle Editions Ltd.

Printed and bound in the United States of America

Contents

	Preface	4
	Acknowledgments	5
Chapter 1	Beginnings: 1936–1939	6
Chapter 2	The Western Campaign: January–June 1940	15
Chapter 3	The Battle of Britain: July 1940–February 1941	22
Chapter 4	7/JG 26 In The Mediterranean Theater: February–August 1941	38
Chapter 5	The Channel Front: 1941	49
Chapter 6	The Abbeville Boys: 1942	65
Chapter 7	Germany Loses The Air War: January 1943–May 1944	92
	Color Plates	97
Chapter 8	The Invasion Front: June–December 1944	131
Chapter 9	The Final Battles: 1945	148
Chapter 10	Camouflage And Markings	156
Appendices	Sources	164
	Table Of Equivalent Ranks—GAF, USAAF, and RAF	165
	Glossary	166
	Index	168

Preface

World War II was arguably the most significant event in the first nine decades of our century. The war and its immediate aftermath determined the nature of the world in which most of us grew up. The battle between the Luftwaffe and the air forces of the Western Allies—the Royal Air Force (RAF) and later the US Army Air Forces (USAAF)—for supremacy over the skies of Western Europe continued for the entire war, from 1939 to 1945. This remains the world's most important aerial campaign in terms of scale, length, and ultimate result. The Luftwaffe lost this campaign; indeed, it fell from a position of European dominance to virtual extinction in the brief period of one year. The Jagdwaffe, or German fighter arm, lost more than 100 percent of its strength in pilots, and with them almost all of its effectiveness, during this year, and its history has all of the elements of a classical tragedy. The above is offered as a partial explanation for the continued fascination that the Luftwaffe asserts on the Western mind.

The fortunes of Jagdgeschwader 26 (JG 26) mirrored those of the Luftwaffe—and Germany—as a whole. This unit has a special appeal for the historian and enthusiast. It was considered the best fighter unit in the Luftwaffe for most of the war, and it was therefore based in Western Europe, where it opposed the best Allied air forces. The Allies knew JG 26 well and nicknamed it "The Abbeville Boys" as a mark of their respect. Although this author's narrative history of JG 26 has recently been published in English (*JG 26: Top Guns of the Luftwaffe*, Orion Books, New York, 1991), the present book, a pictorial history, does not compete with it, but takes a different approach. The objective of this book is to tell the story of JG 26 through a selection of photographs and paintings, using only sufficient text to provide continuity. These visual images evoke a sense of immediacy and reality quite different from the mood attainable from words alone.

Most of the photographs are from private collections and have never before been published. The remainder, primarily from government sources such as the German Bundesarchiv, are reprinted here without apology; first, because they are needed for adequate coverage; second, for their unsurpassed quality; and third, because many can now be identified correctly for the first time. The photograph collection of the Bundesarchiv has never been captioned—it has only a minimal index—and accurate captions are necessary if anything resembling true history is to result from a melange of photographs.

Any book of this size and scope will contain errors, for which I apologize. I welcome correspondence with anyone who has corrections or other information to share pertaining to this fascinating period in aviation history. There is one aspect of the history of JG 26 that has not yet appeared in print—the tables of missions, bases, commanders, claims, and losses that support the historian's descriptions, inferences, and conclusions. A "JG 26 War Diary" is planned to fill this gap.

Donald L. Caldwell
Lake Jackson, Texas
June 1993

Acknowledgments

This work would not have been possible without the generous cooperation of the veterans of the Geschwader. Their enthusiasm for the project is apparently undiminished after an eight-year deluge of requests from the United States for information and material. The men whose photographs appear in this book are: Herr Balloff, F. W. Bauerhenne, Karl Boehm-Tettelbach, Matthias Buchmann, Joseph Buerschgens, Peter Crump, Helmut Doelling, Georg Eder (deceased), Xaver Ellenrieder, Adolf Galland, Heinz Gehrke, Georg Genth, Adolf Glunz, Georg Kiefner, Hans Kukla, Ernst Laube, Erwin Leykauf, Fritz Losigkeit, Werner Molge, Johannes Naumann, Josef Niesmak, Rolf Pingel, Heinrich Schild, Gottfried Schmidt, Friedrich Schneider (deceased), Gerhard Schoepfel, Rolf Schroedter (deceased), Waldemar Soeffing (deceased), Otto Stammberger, Gerhard Strasen, Walter Stumpf, Siegfried Sy (deceased), Fritz Ungar, and Gerd Wiegand. Families of the following deceased veterans also provided photographs: Artur Beese, Karl-Heinz Kempf, Josef Priller, Herr Reimers, and Bernhard Wollnitz.

A special acknowledgment is owed to Chris Thomas for his incomparable paintings, which I believe set a new standard for Luftwaffe art.

The fraternity of air-war historians and enthusiasts has continued to give me its unstinting support. Photographs were supplied by: Arno Abendroth, Bernd Barbas, Johan Breugelmans, A. J. Cranston, Jim Crow, Cynrick De Decker, Joachim Eickhoff, Carl Hildebrandt, Jean-Yves Lorant, Michael Meyer, Eric Mombeek, Michael Payne, Gert Poelchau (deceased), Jean-Louis Roba, Guenter Sundermann, Helmut Terbeck, Chris Thomas, and Lothair Vanoverbeke. Information, advice, and/or photographic assistance was obtained from Winfried Bock, John Campbell, Jerry Crandall, Peter Ebert, Russ Fahey, Larry Hickey, Jim Kitchens, George Morrison, Lorenz Rasse, John Smith III, Sam Sox, Etienne Vanackere, and Dominique van den Broucke.

Veterans of the USAAF were also of great help, and I would like to thank former bomber pilots Elmer Clarey and Robert Seelos for the use of their photographs.

The following archives have granted permission to reprint photographs from their collections: the Bundesarchiv-Bildarchiv (Koblenz), the Canadian Public Archives, the établissement Cinématographique et Photographique des Armées, the National Air & Space Museum, and the United States Air Force Museum.

Last but by no means least, my thanks go to my wife Jackie and my daughters for their patience and support.

Chapter 1

Beginnings: 1936–1939

Jagdgeschwader (fighter wing) 26, or JG 26, had its origin in the Third Gruppe (group) of JG 134 (abbreviated III/JG 134). This Gruppe was ordered to Cologne on 7 March 1936 as the fighter component of the small force sent west by Adolf Hitler to reoccupy the German states along the country's western border. The German armed forces were still tiny—the Luftwaffe had been es-

tablished only one year before, on 1 March 1935—but the Allies failed to respond, and the Gruppe settled in with its He 51 fighters at the Cologne civil airport, beginning an association with the lower Rhineland that was to last for the nine years of JG 26's existence. A new Geschwader headquarters, Jagdgeschwader 234, and a new Gruppe, II/JG 234, were established at Duesseldorf

The He 51B of the first Kommandeur of I/JG 234 (later I/JG 26), Hptm. Oskar Dinort, on the firing stand at Cologne-Ostheim in early 1937. The First Gruppe's chief armorer, Fw. Kuehn, is on the left. *Meyer*

He 51Bs of 2/JG 234 (later 2/JG 26) on field maneuvers in July 1937. *Meyer*

The Ar 68s of II/JG 234 (later II/JG 26) during an inspection at Duesseldorf in 1937. *Meyer*

in early 1937, and with the redesignation of the Cologne Gruppe as I/JG 234 the Geschwader attained a state of organization that stayed constant for the next two years. Each Gruppe administered three sequentially numbered Staffeln (squadrons): I/JG 234 contained the 1st, 2nd, and 3rd Staffeln, while II/JG 234 contained the 4th, 5th, and 6th. The Geschwader was equipped with the Luftwaffe's two standard biplane fighters. The First Gruppe flew the Heinkel He 51; the Second Gruppe, the Arado Ar 68.

The Geschwader began receiving Messerschmitt Bf 109Bs in November 1937 and was the second Luftwaffe unit to equip fully with the new monoplane fighter, at that time the most advanced in the world. The unit's ties to JG 134 were not fully severed until November 1938, when JG 234 obtained its first Kommodore, Obst. Eduard Ritter von Schleich, a highly-respected and successful World War I fighter pilot. The Geschwader was renumbered that same month as JG 132, a designation that lasted less than a year. The unit was also awarded an honor title; on 11 December 1938 the Geschwader became Jagdgeschwader 132 "Schlageter." The name of Albert Leo Schlageter was well-known in the Rhineland; he had been executed by the French army in 1923 after blowing up a section of railroad track to protest the reparations policies of the Allied occupying forces. Honor titles were but rarely bestowed in the Luftwaffe, and this one served to reinforce the ties between the Geschwader and the area in which it was based. On 1 May 1939 the unit was renumbered for the last time, its official designation becoming Jagdgeschwader 26 "Schlageter." The Geschwader emblem, a black gothic "S" in a white shield, was painted on all aircraft and much of the ground equipment.

JG 26 did not take part in the German invasion of Poland that precipitated World War II, but remained in a defensive posture along Germany's western border. Both Gruppen relocated west of the Rhine, the First to Odendorf and the Second to Boenninghardt, but since its bases were opposite the neutral countries of Belgium and the Netherlands, and British and French aircraft rarely strayed that far north, the Geschwader saw little combat during the Sitzkrieg or "sitting war" that lasted from September 1939 until Germany's invasion of France and the Low Countries in May 1940. The Geschwader continued to patrol, train, and reorganize. The Third Gruppe of the Geschwader was established at Werl in September, and its 7th, 8th, and 9th Staffeln brought the Geschwader up to full establishment strength of three Gruppen, nine Staffeln, and about 120 Bf 109E fighters. In December, Obst. von Schleich passed command of the Geschwader to Maj. Hans-Hugo Witt.

A tenth Staffel, an *ad hoc* night fighting organization designated 10(Nacht)/JG 26, was set up hurriedly in September and equipped with a variety of obsolete aircraft. It was unsuccessful in its night-fighting role and was sent to northern Germany to bolster the air defenses of the naval bases. Ironically, while there, the Staffel scored the Geschwader's first major successes of the war, in the so-called Battle of the German Bight, a defeat for the Royal Air Force (RAF) that soured the British on the idea of attacking targets in Germany by day. Very soon after this battle, 10(Nacht)/JG 26 was absorbed in a specialized night-fighting Gruppe and left JG 26. Unfortunately, no publishable photographs from 10(Nacht)/JG 26 could be found for this book.

The photographs illustrating this chapter show the major aspects of the Geschwader's peacetime existence —base routine, maneuvers, and inspections.

Men of II/JG 234 relax during one of the many 1937 field maneuvers. The 4th Staffel's Bf 109Bs are parked in front of the Second Gruppe's remaining Ar 68s. *Meyer*

Hptm. Walter Grabmann, Kommandeur of I/JG 234, in his Bf 109B at Cologne-Ostheim in 1938. *Boehm-Tettelbach*

Bf 109Bs of II/JG 234 at Duesseldorf in 1938. *Meyer*

Bf 109Bs of I/JG 234 at Cologne-Ostheim in 1938. *Meyer*

Pilots of 1/JG 234, photographed during a firing exercise on a North Sea island during 1938. From left: unknown; Lt. Leppla; Oblt. Karl Boehm-Tettelbach, the Staffelkapitaen; Lt. Unger; unknown; unknown. *Boehm-Tettelbach*

Sixth Staffel Bf 109Cs on field maneuvers in 1938. *Meyer*

A Bf 109E-1 of the 4th Staffel, known as the Adamsonstaffel for its emblem, the cartoon character Adamson, airborne over Germany in the summer of 1939. "White 15" carried the Staffel insignia beneath the left side of the cockpit. At this time, the Staffel was part of the Second Gruppe; later in 1939 it joined the new Third Gruppe, and in 1943 it moved to the First. *Meyer*

Genmaj. Eduard Ritter von Schleich, JG 26's first Kommodore. *Meyer*

The 6th Staffel during the last prewar maneuvers, 10 August 1939. Note the white temporary markings on the tail and wing tip of "Yellow 12." *Doelling via Rasse*

An early form of the 2nd Staffel's Red Devil insignia, photographed on a Bf 109E-1 during a live firing exercise on the Island of Sylt in early 1939. *Buchmann*

The 6th Staffel's Fw. Franz Lueders (POW 21 Jun 41) in the cockpit of his "Yellow 7" at Oerlinghausen on 11 August 1939. *Doelling via Rasse*

Maj. Ernst Freiherr von Berg, Third Gruppe Kommandeur from November 1939 to June 1940, photographed beside his Bf 109E during the winter of 1939–40. *Meyer*

Lt. Josef Buerschgens, the Geschwader's first combat casualty, is visited in the hospital by his Kapitaen, Oblt. Fritz Losigkeit, in late 1939. *Buerschgens*

A 9th Staffel Bf 109E-1 at Muehlheim-Essen during the Sitzkrieg of late 1939. Note the early Hellhound insignia beneath the cockpit. *Glunz*

A 1st Staffel Bf 109E at the unit's second wartime base, Dortmund. The Staffel was based at Dortmund from November 1939 to January 1940. The Staffel's Grasshopper insignia is just visible beneath the cockpit. *Meyer*

9th Staffel Bf 109E-1s photographed at Muehlheim-Essen during late 1939. Note the very large wing insignia, ordered by the RLM after incidents of "friendly fire" during the Polish campaign. *Glunz*

The 9th Staffel's Uffz. Artur Beese (KIA 6 Feb 44) with his two ground crewmen. The caption on the back of this photo, in his own hand, states that he had been given aircraft number "11," his lucky number. *Beese via Roba*

The 2nd Staffel's Lt. Martin Rysavy (KIA 2 Jul 41) stands beside his belly-landed "Red 6" in the winter of 1939–40. *Meyer*

Three 4th Staffel pilots pose stiffly with one of the unit's Bf 109E-3s in early 1939. *Sundermann*

Chapter 2

The Western Campaign: January–June 1940

The Geschwader's first clue that the Luftwaffe was preparing for offensive warfare on the Western Front came in the form of an order in early 1940 to repaint all its aircraft. The black-green/dark green segmented camouflage scheme of its Messerschmitts was highly effective when seen from above against the background of Germany's forests, but was of no value in air-to-air combat. The Staffeln were ordered to repaint their Bf 109E-1s and Bf 109E-3s. The light blue undersurface color was extended up the sides of the aircraft, and the upper plan view surfaces were lightened by replacing one of the dark greens in the segmented pattern with green-gray. All aircraft now decked out in fresh war paint, the unit was ready to go to war.

After several postponements, the western campaign got underway on 10 May. The Geschwader was still based in the northern sector of the Western Front, and its first task was to support Army Group B's invasion of the Netherlands. It did this by means of freie Jagden or "free hunts," which were fighter sweeps in front of the battle lines, and Jagdschutze or "fighter protection" missions, patrols of sections of the front. Air superiority was won on the first day. The Netherlands surrendered after five days of heavy fighting, and the Geschwader moved to Belgium, still in support of Army Group B. In the meantime Army Group A had secretly penetrated the Ardennes, split the French and British armies, and was racing toward the English Channel.

JG 26 was among the first Luftwaffe fighter units to engage the RAF over Dunkirk, the small French port from which the British planned to withdraw their army. After battling the British Spitfires and Hurricanes for the eight days of the evacuation, the Geschwader moved to airfields in the Calais area and paused briefly to regroup. Hptm. Adolf Galland arrived from JG 27 on 6 June to take command of the Third Gruppe, an event that proved to be of great significance for the future of the Geschwader. JG 26 was next directed to the south, in support of the army's attack on the main force of the French Army. The French defenses quickly broke, and the Geschwader followed the advance southward, finally stopping at Villacoublay, a large permanent French base outside Paris. The Second Gruppe was given the

In October 1939 these ground crews transferred from the First Gruppe to the newly formed Third Gruppe at Werl. In November they moved to Muehlheim as part of the 7th Staffel. Here they await assignment to the day's work details. The Staffel's Red Heart insignia can be seen beneath the cockpit—Muehlheim-Essen, early 1940. *Buchmann*

Lt. Eberhard Henrici's 1st Staffel Bf 109E "White 13" at Diepholz in February. *Meyer*

"Black 1," the Bf 109E-3 of Oblt. Kuno Wendt, Kapitaen of the 8th Staffel, the Adamsonstaffel, at Muehlheim shortly before the invasion of France. *Genth*

honor of flying cover patrols over the armistice negotiations at Compiegne. Command of the Geschwader passed from Maj. Witt to Maj. Gotthardt Handrick, famous throughout Germany as the winner of the modern pentathlon in the 1936 Olympics in Berlin. After the Armistice was signed on 22 June, the Geschwader quickly moved back to its permanent bases in Germany, to rest and refit for what all personnel knew would be the next campaign—the invasion of England.

The photographs capture something of the Geschwader's routine during the first winter and spring of the war. The practice of painting Staffel emblems on the aircraft reached full fruition during the period, and the emblems show up well on the newly lightened fuselage sides. Most of these photos were taken during the last days of the Sitzkrieg; the hectic six-week Blitzkrieg was poorly documented in writing or photographs by the overworked men of the Geschwader, which was inadequately staffed or equipped for a war of movement.

The Bf 109E-3 of JG 26's second Kommodore, Maj. Hans-Hugo Witt, photographed in the spring of 1940. The Ritter (knight) has been reported to have been Witt's personal emblem, but it appeared on several other aircraft of the Geschwaderstab. The chevron and pointed horizontal bar were parts of the standard tactical sign used by JG 26's Kommodoren. *Meyer*

Maj. Witt airborne in his Bf 109E-3. *Meyer*

Oblt. Fritz Losigkeit, Kapitaen of the 2nd Staffel, exits his aircraft. *Meyer*

The emblems of the three Third Gruppe Staffeln on the rudder of a Bf 109E, probably that of its mid-1940 Kommandeur, Maj. Ernst Freiherr von Berg. From the top, the emblems represent the 7th, 8th, and 9th Staffeln. *Schmidt*

17

"Red 16," a Bf 109E flown by the 2nd Staffel's Kapitaen, Oblt. Losigkeit, in the spring of 1940. Note the red command pennant on the antenna. *Meyer*

The Bf 109E-3 of the Geschwader adjutant, Oblt. Hasselmann—photographed in early 1940. *Meyer*

Flg. Guenter Blotko (KIA 19 Jul 40), dressed as the traditional Easter rabbit, strikes a pose during the proclamation of the 1940 holiday program. Standing at the left of the group of three officers in the center is Lt. Walter Blume (POW 18 Aug 40). *Buchmann*

Pilots of the Third Gruppe await orders at Chievres during the western campaign. Clockwise from left: Lt. Josef Haiboeck, Lt. Johannes "Hans" Naumann, Lt. Joachim Muencheberg (KIA 23 Mar 1943), Fw. Bernhard Eberz (KIA 25 Jul 40). *Schoepfel*

Oblt. Walter Horten, Geschwader technical officer, sits on his spotless Bf 109E during the spring of 1940. *Meyer*

The 4th Staffel's Bf 109E "White 3," W.Nr. 779, after a belly-landing during the French campaign. Note the out-of-proportion fuselage insignia. *Cranston*

The 5th Staffel's Bf 109E-1 "Black 5," photographed amidst the detritus of the Western campaign. *Meyer*

The 6th Staffel's Bf 109E-1 "Brown 9," W.Nr. 1937, after force-landing in France on 1 June. *Doelling via Rasse*

The 6th Staffel's "Brown 2" at Dieppe in June. *Meyer*

A Schwarm of 4th Staffel Bf 109E-1s and E-3s, led by the Kapitaen, Hptm. Karl Ebbighausen (KIA 16 Aug 40)—photographed after the conclusion of the French campaign. *Meyer*

A captured French Morane-Saulnier MS 406 fighter, photographed by a Second Gruppe ground crewman. *Reimers via Ebert*

Chapter 3

The Battle of Britain:
July 1940–February 1941

While in Germany, nearly all of the Geschwader's remaining Bf 109E-1s were fitted with seat and back armor and most had their lightly framed canopies replaced with heavier units containing armored glass. The unsuccessful Bf 109E-3s disappeared from the JG 26 inventory, and Bf 109E-4s began arriving from the Messerschmitt factory in the new standard camouflage scheme of dark green/green-gray segments over light blue sides and undersurfaces. This model was fully combat-worthy, with an armament of two machine guns and two machine cannons, and built-in cockpit armor.

JG 26 was ordered back to France on 21 July 1940, moving onto fields within a few miles of the English Channel at Calais. It flew its first missions over England on 24 July. Although equipped with a fighter at least the equal of the RAF's best, the Spitfire, and boasting the most effective offensive formations and tactics of any air force in the world, the German Jagdwaffe (fighter force) was unable to assert a decisive influence over England. Its freie Jagden were only successful when enemy aircraft could be enticed to do battle. RAF Fighter Command,

with the benefit of superior radar and ground control and a strong-willed commander, was able to conserve its strength for use against its most dangerous opponents, the German bombers. The Jagdwaffe was forced to assume a new mission, bomber escort, for which it possessed neither the doctrine nor the discipline. Only a few Gruppenkommandeure (group commanders) were able to carry out escort missions with consistent success. Galland's Third Gruppe compiled an outstanding record, and he was rewarded on 22 August with command of the entire Geschwader. He immediately began to put up escort missions in full Geschwader strength, at that time a novelty. Galland's new command soon gained a reputation as the best escort unit in the Jagdwaffe. The escort formations and tactics he devised were widely accepted and standardized by the Luftwaffe, but for full effectiveness these required many more fighters than the Germans possessed.

Cursed by poor intelligence and their own indecisiveness, Hitler and Goering switched targets on 7 Sep-

A Bf 109E on the 7th Staffel armorers' test stand in the early summer. From left: an unidentified aircraft mechanic, Gefr. Langhammer, Gefr. Baumgart, and Fw. Kothe. *Buchmann*

A lunchtime conference at the Third Gruppe airfield in Caffiers, summer 1940. From left, front row: Maj. Adolf Galland, Third Gruppe Kommandeur; Maj. Gotthardt Handrick, Kommodore from 24 June 1940 to 21 August 1940; rear row: Hptm. Wilde, Geschwader operations officer; Lt. Muencheberg, Gruppe adjutant; Oblt. Hasselmann, Geschwader adjutant. *Schoepfel*

Geschwaderstab ground crewmen Gefr. Olemotz and Ogfr. Thoma pose at Audembert with Oblt. Horten's Bf 109E-4. *Meyer*

Oblt. Gustav "Micky" Sprick's ground crew adjust the armament of his Bf 109E. His crew chief, Fw. F. W. Bauerhenne, is seated in the cockpit. Sprick became 8th Staffel Kapitaen on 8 August, and flew this "Black 1" for a short period before adopting "Black 13." *Schmidt*

tember from the RAF's vulnerable airfields and air defense network to the world's largest city, London. The RAF recovered strength quickly, and able now to concentrate in defense of a single target, pummeled the German day bombers. All hope of a quick victory gone, the German bomber force turned to night bombing, leaving the day fighters no missions other than ineffective freie Jagden and even more fruitless level bombing missions with Bf 109E-4/Bs, each carrying a single 250kg (551lb) bomb. Day activity petered out with the arrival of the rains of late autumn; JG 26 was forced to abandon its muddy coastal fields for the relative altitude and good drainage of Abbeville-Drucat, near the mouth of the Somme River. Adolf Hitler, on a rare visit to the front, spent Christmas day at Geschwader headquarters in an Abbeville chateau. Finally, on 9 February 1941, JG 26 was ordered back to Germany to rest and refit, the last rest period granted to the Geschwader as a whole for the entire war. Under Galland's leadership, JG 26 had become the Luftwaffe's premier fighter unit, an evaluation confirmed by Goering in a 1941 speech. Its reward was to be posted in the west for the rest of the war, facing the Allies' most capable air forces.

The Bf 109E-1 of Oblt. Werner Bartels, Third Gruppe technical officer, which had been shot down over Margate on 24 July 1940 and put on display at Croydon, England. *Cranston*

The Bf 109E of Oblt. Hasselmann, Geschwader adjutant, photographed in Audembert, summer 1940. *Meyer*

Aircraft of the JG 26 Geschwaderstab; Maj. Handrick's "Top Hat" is on the left. Photographed at Audembert, summer 1940. *Meyer*

The 7th Staffel's Lt. Gerhard Mueller-Duehe stands beside the Spitfire of Plt. Off. Ralph Roberts of the Royal Air Force's No. 54 Sqd., whom he had just shot down near Calais. The date is 15 August; Mueller-Duehe was killed over England three days later. *Bundesarchiv*

The photographs illustrate some of the notable incidents and leading personnel of this period. Photographs and especially the paintings have been selected to show the evolution of aircraft markings. Very early in the Battle of Britain, the Jagdwaffe decided to use yellow tactical markings to aid quick identification in the air. These progressed from yellow-tipped wings, rudders, and elevators to full yellow rudders and engine cowlings. At the same time, the Messerschmitts' light blue fuselage sides were felt to be too conspicuous and were toned down by overcoats of green-gray or gray paint.

Conference of Third Gruppe officers at Caffiers. From left: Oblt. Josef Haiboeck, adjutant; Oblt. Muencheberg, 7th Staffel Kapitaen; Lt. Buerschgens (POW 1 Sep 40), 7th Staffel; Oblt. Micky Sprick (KIA 28 Jun 41), 8th Staffel Kap- itaen; Oblt. Heinz Ebeling (POW 5 Nov 40), 9th Staffel Kap- itaen, who is carrying a cased flask of cognac just awarded for his latest victory. *Schoepfel*

One of Maj. Galland's Third Gruppe aircraft in a highly non- standard mottled gray camouflage. It displays twenty-two vic- tory bars, dating the photograph as mid-August. *Buchmann*

The tail of Lt. Josef Buerschgens' 7th Staffel Bf 109E-1, pho- tographed on 18 August 1940. It displays nine victory bars and the new theater marking—a yellow rudder tip. *Meyer*

Activity on the airfield momentarily interrupts Maj. Galland's briefing of his Third Gruppe officers in mid-August. Those visible, from left: Gruppe flight surgeon, Oblt. Gerhard Schoepfel, Oblt. Georg Beyer (POW 28 Aug 40), Lt. Mueller-Duehe (KIA 18 Aug 40), Lt. Buerschgens, Maj. Galland, Lt. Hans Christinnecke (with life jacket) (POW 6 Sep 40), Lt. Sprick, Lt. Muencheberg, unknown, Hptm. Dr. Rolf Schroedter (technical officer—with glasses). *Buerschgens*

Oblt. Schoepfel's four victories of 18 August 1940 are recorded on his Messerschmitt. These bars commemorated his most noteworthy battle—the single-handed destruction of four No. 501 Sqd. (RAF) Hurricanes. A few days later Schoepfel was given command of the Third Gruppe. *Schoepfel*

Lt. Buerschgens in his Bf 109E-1 in August. Its cockpit still lacks head armor. Buerschgens was shot down on 1 September—by a German fighter—and spent the rest of the war in a Canadian POW camp. *Meyer*

Adamson, the well-known symbol of the 8th Staffel, heads for the latrine with a copy of the *Times*. Photographed in Caffiers, summer 1940. *Bauerhenne*

Two aircraft of the 1st Staffel, Oblt. Eberhard Henrici's "White 13" and Oblt. Franz Hoernig's "White 1," prepare to take off from Audembert. Henrici replaced Hoernig as Staffelkapitaen on 9 September and was killed by Spitfires on 17 November. *Meyer*

A 9th Staffel Bf 109E after a forced landing by Fw. Artur Beese at St. Inglevert, France, on 24 August. The weakest point of the Messerschmitt fighter's fuselage was just behind the cockpit. *Cranston*

Oblt. Muencheberg, 7th Staffel Kapitaen, prepares for another sortie. Photographed in Caffiers, mid-September. *Buchmann*

The Third Gruppe scrap yard at Caffiers in the summer of 1940. *Meyer*

Oblt. Schoepfel, 9th Staffel Kapitaen, ponders a point in front of the mapboard. Photographed in Caffiers, August 1940. *Schoepfel*

Eighth Staffel Bf 109Es prepare to take off on a mission during mid-August. Note the triangular yellow identification marking on the rudder of the second aircraft. *Schmidt via Mombeek*

Ninth Staffel pilots relax outside their duty pilots' trailer; note the local equivalent of a soft drink machine beside the door. From left: Oblt. Schoepfel, Fw. Willy Fronhoefer (POW 31 Aug 40), Uffz. Heinrich Humburg, Lt. Josef Haiboeck. Photographed in Caffiers, August 1940. *Schoepfel*

The "weapon-yodeling team" of the 7th Staffel in front of their workplace. Front row, from left: Gefr. Stoeckl, Uffz. Siebert, Fw. Kothe, Flg. Maeder, Uffz. Hagedorn. Behind them, from left, Gefr. Langhammer and an unidentified reservist. *Buchmann*

A little-known Bf 109E of Maj. Galland, W.Nr. 5398, photographed at Audembert in early September with twenty-nine victory bars on their original blue surround on an otherwise-yellow rudder. *Meyer*

Uffz. Heinz Bock's 7th Staffel "White 2" after crashing at Rye, England, on 17 September. The small identity number and bar were characteristic of Third Gruppe aircraft throughout the Battle. *Meyer*

The 6th Staffel Kapitaen, Oblt. Walter Schneider, in his "Brown 1." Note the supplemental armored windshield. Photographed in Marquise, late summer. *Doelling via Rasse*

Maj. Galland is congratulated following his 40th victory. In the circle at center, from left: Hptm. Viktor Causin, ground executive (with cognac); Oblt. Rothenberg (Galland's adjutant); Uffz. Meyer (Galland's crew chief); two correspondents; and

Maj. Galland. The aircraft is that of Oblt. Horten, the technical officer, and bears the minimal JG 26 Geschwaderstab marking: a pointed horizontal bar before and a horizontal bar behind the fuselage cross. *Bundesarchiv*

Oblt. Sprick, 8th Staffel Kapitaen, in the cockpit of his Bf 109E-4/N during the autumn of 1940—most likely on 28 September, after his twentieth victory, which would explain the crowd. *Schmidt*

The Bf 109E-4/N of the 4th Staffel's Uffz. Horst Perez, photographed on a Defense Bond tour in the United States in 1941 after its forced landing at Eastbourne, England, on 30 September 1940. The aircraft was formerly assigned to Hptm. Ebbighausen and carries five of his victory markings on the fin. *Air Force Museum*

The 2nd Staffel staff coupe photographed in Audembert, late summer. *Meyer*

On his return to Audembert after scoring his fortieth victory on 23 September, Maj. Galland is greeted first by his crew chief, Uffz. Meyer. Note that Galland's W.Nr. 5819 did not display his Mickey Mouse insignia on this day. *Bundesarchiv*

Uffz. Perez's "White 4" on display in Canada in 1941. *Cranston*

Oblt. Losigkeit's Bf 109E-4 "Red 1" after a forced landing off a French beach in the autumn of 1940; note the early unarmored canopy. Losigkeit left the Geschwader in May 1941 to become the German military attaché in Tokyo. *Cranston*

The 7th Staffel ground crewmen's living quarters on the field at Caffiers, complete with a good-luck stork nesting in a fake chimney. *Bundesarchiv*

A 2nd Staffel Bf 109E-7, the first Bf 109 model to carry a drop tank, photographed in late 1940. *Meyer*

The 8th Staffel ground crewmen's living quarters at Caffiers. *Bundesarchiv*

The 5th Staffel's "Black 11" after suffering a collapsed landing gear. Photographed in Marquise, autumn 1940. *Reimers via Ebert*

The 2nd Staffel's Bf 109E-1 "Red 3" is set back on its landing gear. The feathered prop blades denote a forced landing, rather than landing gear failure. Photographed in Abbeville, 23 December 1940. *Bundesarchiv*

Christmas 1940 at the Chateau Bonnance in Abbeville. From left: Hptm. Rolf Pingel, Adolf Hitler, Obstlt. Galland, Hptm. Schoepfel. *Schoepfel*

Fw. Bruno Hegenauer of the JG 26 Stabsschwarm exits his Bf 109E-4 at Abbeville on 23 December. Note the green spinner tip. This aircraft has often been misidentified as Galland's W.Nr. 5819, but lacks the latter's wing cameras. *Bundesarchiv*

The Bf 109E-4 of the First Gruppe Kommandeur, Hptm. Rolf Pingel, photographed during the winter of 1940–41. The aircraft displays many interesting markings details: two white bands on a blue spinner; an all-yellow cowl and rudder; a row of flags under the canopy sill; and seventeen red victory bars, with roundels above the bottom seven. *Cranston*

Obstlt. Galland taxies his Bf 109E-4/N on 23 December. The narrow gravel taxi strip at Abbeville, hastily put down to keep the aircraft out of the mud, must have posed a challenge to every Bf 109 pilot. *Bundesarchiv*

Obstlt. Galland (white coveralls) has just returned to Audembert from an early December mission. *Doelling via Rasse*

Chapter 4

7/JG 26 In The Mediterranean Theater: February–August 1941

In December 1940 the Luftwaffe was forced to send a number of heavy fighters, dive bombers, and medium bombers to the Mediterranean to shore up the Italian air force. No single-engined fighters were included in this first wave, but in mid-January 1941 it was decided to supplement the force with a small number of Bf 109s. One of JG 26's nine Staffeln was recalled early from home leave and ordered south. The unit chosen was the 7th "Red Heart" Staffel, under the command of Oblt. Joachim Muencheberg. It reached Sicily in early February; its new Bf 109E-7s first made their presence felt over Malta on 12 February, by shooting down three Hurricanes. By the end of the month, this single Staffel had achieved unchallenged air supremacy over the island and its now-demoralized British defenders.

The Axis powers passed up an opportunity to conquer Malta cheaply and instead turned their attention to the Balkans, where the Italian invaders of Greece were being routed. The entire Luftwaffe force on Sicily, including 7/JG 26, flew to Italy in early April to support the German attack on Yugoslavia. Muencheberg's unit returned to Sicily two days later, but only a single Gruppe of dive bombers accompanied them. The Luftwaffe raids on Malta resumed, but lacked the strength to force a conclusion.

In late May, the 7th Staffel was ordered to southern Greece, from where it was soon sent to Libya to reinforce I/JG 27, the only Bf 109 unit in North Africa. The Bf 109E-7s of the 7th Staffel were not equipped with sand filters, and replacement engines were hard to obtain. Two months of combat above the desert sands saw the unit's serviceability dwindle to nothing, and in August the men of the Staffel were ordered back to France to rejoin their parent Third Gruppe; the hulks of their aircraft were left behind in the desert.

The exploits of this single Staffel attracted great attention in Germany in 1941 and are still worth noting today. Its record was unmatched in the air war: its pilots scored fifty-two air victories while in the theater, without the loss in combat of a single pilot or airplane. Had

The entire aircraft complement of the 7th Staffel is lined up on an Italian Air Force field in Rome, about two hours before departing for Sicily on 9 February. Note the variations in camouflage. *Buchmann*

A 7th Staffel Bf 109E-7 comes in for a landing on Sicily in February. *Buchmann*

its successes over Malta been followed up with an invasion, the outcome of the war might well have been affected.

Official photographic coverage of the 7th Staffel's sojourn in the Mediterranean theater was excellent—Sicily was undoubtedly good duty for the Propaganda Companies. The events depicted on the surviving rolls of film allow most of the photographs to be dated exactly. The photograph collection of Matthias Buch-mann, an armorer in the 7th Staffel, was made available for this book and supplied valuable additional coverage. Unfortunately, not all of the Staffel's dozen pilots can be identified in the photographs, even though their names are known. Half of these men were lost through death or transfer too soon after their return to France for identified photographs to find their way into the Geschwader records.

Oblt. Joachim Muencheberg in "White 1," very soon after the 7th Staffel's arrival on Sicily. *E.C.P.A.*

The DB 601N engine of "White 6" is serviced on Sicily. *Bundesarchiv*

Pilots' quarters at Gela in late February; note the pinups. *Bundesarchiv*

Oblt. Muencheberg in "White 1," after downing his second Hurricane over Malta. This is not his better-known "White 12", which had the wing-mounted cameras issued only to the Jagdwaffe's top scorers. Photographed in Gela, 16 February. *E.C.P.A.*

Oblt. Muencheberg's return to Gela after his 200th combat sortie on 28 March brought out the cameras of the amateur photographers. Here Lt. Hans Johannsen (KIA 28 March 1942) greets him with the traditional laurel wreath. *Buchmann*

Oblt. Muencheberg is carried from the field by the Staffel's senior non-commissioned officer, Hptfw. Halbmass, and the Staffel clerks. *Buchmann*

Uffz. Georg Mondry (KIA 31 May 1943) demonstrates the technique he used to down his first victim, a No. 261 Sqd. Hurricane, to his ground crewmen. Photographed in Gela, 16 February. *E.C.P.A.*

Oblt. Muencheberg's Bf 109E-7 alongside a Bf 110 of III/ZG 26. Photographed in Sicily, 28 March. *N.A.S.M.*

Oblt. Johannsen impresses a young Fascist during a March tour of Gela airfield by the Ballila Youth. *Bundesarchiv*

Oblt. Klaus Mietusch (KIA 17 Sep 44), gloves in hand and flares in boot, exits his aircraft. *Bundesarchiv*

Obfw. Ernst Laube in the cockpit of his Bf 109E-7 at Gela. This is an often-reproduced photograph, selected here for its clear depiction of the aircraft's North European camouflage scheme. *Bundesarchiv*

Men of the 7th Staffel change a tire at Gela without benefit of a jack. *Bundesarchiv*

The film actress Carola Hoehn visited the Staffel at Gela as part of a theatrical troupe; she is seen here with her mother, as guests of the Kapitaen. *Buchmann*

At the end of May the Staffel transferred to Greece. The fatigue of the long flight shows on the faces of the ground crewmen; from left: Ogfr. Mueller, Uffz. Siebert, Ogfr. Schmidt. *Buchmann*

The Staffel maintenance detachment on a desolate Greek field in June. This is the kitchen; the walls were only to break the wind, as it seldom rained. In the center, the cook's helper; to his right, chief clerk Uffz. Juris. *Buchmann*

A 300-liter auxiliary fuel tank is attached to a Staffel Bf 109E-7 at Gela. *Bundesarchiv*

Seventh Staffel pilots prepare to depart Sicily on 5 April for Italy, from where they will attack Yugoslavia on the following day; Uffz. Mondry, the unit "Spassvogel" (joke-bird), is his typically irrepressible self. *Bundesarchiv*

In late June the members of the Staffel were finally issued tropical kit to replace their woolen uniforms. A bemused Gefr. Matthias Buchmann has not yet adjusted to the lack of itching. *Buchmann*

The 7th Staffel's widely dispersed living area at Ain el Gazala, Libya, in August. *Bundesarchiv*

"White 8" gets its engine changed. Photographed in Libya, summer 1941. *Bundesarchiv*

Typical conditions at Ain el Gazala. By August the aircraft and especially their engines, which lacked sand filters, were totally worn out. *Bundesarchiv*

Lt. Johannsen and the nine non-commissioned pilots of the 7th Staffel after their return to France—Uffz. Mondry attempts to align them vertically. From left: Lt. Johannsen, Obfw. Laube, Obfw. Kuehdorf, unknown, Fw. Karl-Heinz Ehlen (KIFA 29 Apr 42), three unknown, Uffz. Mondry, unknown. *Laube via Roba*

The men of the 7th Staffel are greeted by their Gruppenkommandeur, Hptm. Schoepfel, after their return from North Africa. From left: unknown, Oblt. Mietusch, Hptm. Schoepfel, Oblt. Muencheberg, Oblt. Theo Lindemann. *Laube via Roba*

Oblt. Muencheberg's aircraft shows the effects of the desert sand; several layers of paint have been worn off the fuselage. Photographed in Libya, August 1941. *Bundesarchiv*

A gun-harmonization scene on a field that could badly use policing. Photographed in Libya, summer 1941. *Bundesarchiv*

The remains of a 7th Staffel Bf 109E-7 left behind in Libya in 1941 and photographed by an American serviceman in 1943. *Crow*

Chapter 5

The Channel Front: 1941

After their winter furloughs, the men of the Schlageter Geschwader gathered at their permanent bases in the Rhineland. The Stab and the Third Gruppe were given Bf 109Fs, the latest model of the Messerschmitt fighter. The First Gruppe also started to re-equip with Bf 109Fs, but shortages forced it to retain some of its Bf 109Es until summer. At the end of March, JG 26 received orders to return to France. The Geschwader was first based in Brittany, where it stood guard over the German naval forces at Brest. On 1 June it moved back to the familiar coastal plains around Calais, while JG 2 took its place in Brittany. The rest of the German fighter force in France returned to Germany to prepare for the attack on the Soviet Union, leaving the aerial defense of France to

Hptm. Walter Adolph. A Condor Legion veteran, Adolph transferred into JG 26 in October 1940 to take command of the Second Gruppe. On 18 September 1941 he crashed into the Channel in his FW 190—the Geschwader's first fatality in the type. *Schoepfel*

While in Germany the 9th Staffel converted to new Bf 109F-2s at Bonn-Hangelaar. Here Oblt. Kurt Ruppert (KIA 13 Jun 43) taxies his "Yellow 1." *Stammberger via Roba*

these two Jagdgeschwader, JG 2 and JG 26, and a total of no more than 150 operational Messerschmitt fighters.

In an attempt to support the Russians and force the Luftwaffe to return fighters to France, the RAF began a daylight air offensive using small numbers of Blenheim light bombers to bomb targets just over the French and Belgian coastline. The bombers were escorted by massive formations of Spitfires and Hurricanes. This force was slowly built up in strength, but was never capable of causing serious damage, and the German air defense network along the English Channel was able to keep pace simply by improving its radar and communications facilities and aerial equipment, without calling for reinforcements.

The Bf 109F was slightly superior to the best RAF fighter, the Spitfire V, and the score in the 1941 Channel combats clearly favored the Luftwaffe. German superiority increased toward the end of the year, after the Channel units were selected to debut the Luftwaffe's newest and most capable fighter, the Focke-Wulf FW 190A-1. The Second Gruppe of JG 26 was the first

unit to receive the FW 190, but was forced to introduce it to combat slowly, owing to persistent problems with engine overheating. By October the Focke-Wulf fighter was making its presence felt over the Channel, and on 8 November the RAF ended the year's campaign after a disastrous attack on Lille that cost it thirteen Spitfire pilots; German casualties that day were one pilot killed and one severely injured.

Shortly before the end of the year JG 26 lost its Kommodore. Obst. Galland was ordered to Berlin as General of the Fighter Arm; his replacement as Kommodore of JG 26 was Maj. Gerhard Schoepfel of the Third Gruppe.

The photographs depict the full range of 1941 Geschwader aircraft: the Bf 109Fs of the Stab and the Third Gruppe; the Bf 109E-7s and Bf 109Fs of the First Gruppe; and the Bf 109E-7s and FW 190A-1s of the Second Gruppe. Aircraft from the JG 26 Ergaenzungsgruppe (operational training group) are also shown; several of these had previously seen service with the combat Staffeln.

The Bf 109E-7 "Black 8" of the 5th Staffel's Kapitaen, Oblt. Wolfgang Kosse, photographed at Brest-Guipavas soon after the Geschwader's return to France in the spring of 1941. The Staffel's Hans Huckebein emblem can be seen below the cockpit. *Cranston*

The tail of Obstlt. Galland's Bf 109F-0, showing sixty victory bars, photographed at Brest in April. Note the reinforcing bar above the tailwheel; this was added after the tail assemblies of several prototypes failed in flight. *Reimers via Ebert*

Obstlt. Galland's Bf 109E at Brest in April, displaying sixty victory bars; Galland's brand-new Bf 109F-0 is visible in the background. *Cranston*

The Bf 109E-7 of the 3rd Staffel's Lt. Robert Menge in the spring of 1941. Note the row of flags beneath the cockpit; these represented the European nations in which he had fought. Menge was killed by No. 92 Sqd. (RAF) Spitfires on 14 June 1941. *Meyer*

The 3rd Staffel's Uffz. Friedrich Schneider (left) with Lt. Menge's Bf 109E-7. *Meyer*

Eighth Staffel ground crewmen Balloff, Stegmann, and Goedecker converse with Uffz. Max Martin in front of a Staffel Bf 109F-2—St. Brieuc, Brittany, spring 1941. *Schmidt*

The 9th Staffel's Oblt. Ruppert in his Bf 109F-2 at St. Brieuc in April. Note his yellow command pennant on the radio mast. *Stammberger via Roba*

Uffz. Friedrich Schneider is photographed in a 3rd Staffel Bf 109E-7, "Yellow 11," soon after joining the unit in the spring of 1941. *Meyer*

Hptm. Gerhard Schoepfel, Third Gruppe Kommandeur, at cockpit readiness in his Bf 109F-2 at Liegescourt. *Schoepfel*

Hptm. Schoepfel back on the ground at Liegescourt after leading a combat sortie. *Schoepfel*

Pilots of the 9th Staffel unwind after a mission from Liegescourt in June or early July. From left: Lt. Otto Stammberger, Oblt. Kurt Ruppert, Uffz. Gerhard Oemler (KIA 17 Jul 41), Lt. Johannes Naumann (half-covered), and Gefr. Robert Kleinecke (KIA 14 Jul 41). *Stammberger*

Oblt. Josef "Pips" Priller, 1st Staffel Kapitaen, exits his Bf 109E-7 "White 8". Photographed in St. Omer-Clairmarais, June-July 1941. *Meyer*

A 9th Staffel Bf 109F-2, photographed after the Geschwader's return to the Channel coast in mid-1941. Note the small identity codes. A Schlageter shield and Hollenhund emblem are also present. Soon afterward, JG 26 stopped painting Geschwader and Staffel emblems on its aircraft. *Glunz*

A JG 26 Bf 109F in its shelter at Audembert in the summer
of 1941. *Galland*

Oblt. Micky Sprick, 8th Staffel Kapitaen, seated in his
Bf 109F-2—probably the one in which he was killed on 28
June 1941 when its wing collapsed during a combat ma-
neuver. *Meyer*

Battle damage to Uffz. Friedrich Schneider's 3rd Staffel
Bf 109F. The mechanic is holding a compressed air bottle
which deflected a shell and probably saved Schneider's life.
The bottle was positioned on the left of the parachute and
was used to inflate the life raft during a water landing. Photographed in St. Omer-Clairmarais, summer 1941. *Schneider*

Bader takes leave of his hosts at Audembert. *Buchmann*

The downing of Wing Cdr. Douglas Bader by a JG 26 pilot on 9 August 1941, and Bader's subsequent visit to Geschwader headquarters, were memorable events for all members of the unit. Photos by service photographers and by-standers were circulated freely among JG 26 members and found their way into a number of albums. In center of photo: Galland, interpreter, Causin, Bader. *Buchmann*

The wooden case containing Bader's spare artificial legs, dropped by the Royal Air Force on St. Omer airfield during an air raid. *Buchmann*

The quilted engine cover of Ogfr. Gerhard Vogt's 6th Staffel FW 190A-1 is removed in readiness for takeoff from Moorsele in October. *Bundesarchiv*

Ogfr. Vogt prepares to take off from Moorsele in his FW 190A-1 "Brown 13," W.Nr. 013. *Bundesarchiv*

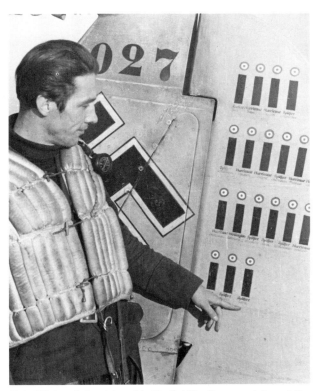

Oblt. Walter Schneider, 6th Staffel Kapitaen, points out the latest victory marking on his FW 190A-1 at Moorsele, Belgium, in September. On a transfer flight to Abbeville on 22 December, Schneider led four aircraft of his Staffel into a hill; all five pilots were killed. *Bundesarchiv*

The 5th Staffel's Lt. Horst Sternberg at Moorsele in October, with one of the first FW 190A-1s in service. Sternberg became Kapitaen of the Staffel on 3 January 1943 and served until he was killed by American 4th Fighter Group P-47s on 22 February 1944. *Lorant via Crow*

Hptm. Johann Schmid, 8th Staffel Kapitaen. Schmid had a meteoric career with JG 26, scoring forty-five victories in 137 missions before crashing to his death in the Channel on 6 November. *Stammberger via Roba*

Oblt. Schneider's FW 190A-1 takes off from Wevelghem, Belgium, in November. *Barbas*

Oblt. Priller prepares to exit from his Bf 109F-2 "White 1" under the lens of the Propaganda Company photographer. All of Priller's aircraft displayed the ace of hearts as a personal emblem and were named *Jutta* after Priller's wife. Photographed in St. Omer-Arques, 25 November. *Bundesarchiv*

Lt. Sternberg prepares to take off from Wevelghem in his "Black 13" on 25 November. *Bundesarchiv*

Second Gruppe FW 190A-1s share their Moorsele taxi strip with a Belgian farm cart. Photographed in October 1941. *E.C.P.A.*

Obst. Adolf Galland's change-of-command ceremony featured Reichsmarschall Goering and Galland's two uniquely-armed Bf 109F-2/U "Specials"—Audembert, 5 December. *E.C.P.A.*

The 6th Staffel's "Brown 1," W.Nr. 033. Obfw. Kurt Goerbig was killed in this aircraft on 22 December. Photographed at Wevelghem on 25 November. *Bundesarchiv*

"Brown 3," a 6th Staffel FW 190A-1, photographed at Wevelghem in November. The erste Wart (crew chief) stands on the wing; the Waffen-Feldwebel (chief armorer), on the ground. *Naumann via Roba*

Obst. Galland's wing cannon-armed Bf 109F-2/U is in the foreground of this photo taken during the change-of-command ceremony. *E.C.P.A.*

Uffz. Friedrich Schneider with a former 4th Staffel Bf 109E-1, W.Nr. 678, now in the JG 26 Ergaenzungsgruppe. Photographed in Cognac, early 1941. *Meyer*

Uffz. Schneider stands by the tail of the ex-4th Staffel Bf 109E-1 in which he received his operational readiness training. Photographed in Cognac, early 1941. *Meyer*

Reichsmarschall Goering notes the victory tally on one of Obst. Galland's Bf 109F-2/Us—Audembert, 5 December. *E.C.P.A.*

Adolf Galland, while on a hunting trip, relaxes with a traditional hunter's pipe instead of his usual cigar. *Genth*

A Bf 109E-7 of the JG 26 Ergaenzungsgruppe, photographed at Rotterdam-Waalhaven in 1941. *Meyer*

Adolf Galland's famous Bf 109E, W.Nr. 5819, now assigned to the Kommandeur of the JG 26 Ergaenzungsgruppe, Oblt. Freiherr von Holtey. Photographed in Cognac, 1941. *Meyer*

Joachim Muencheberg in his tropical khaki jacket. Muencheberg was always a popular photographic subject. *Schmidt*

A smashed Ergaenzungsgruppe Bf 109E at Cognac. *Meyer*

63

Close-up of "White 12," a Bf 109E-7 of the Ergaenzungs-gruppe. *Meyer*

A Bf 109E and pilots of the JG 26 Ergaenzungsgruppe pho-tographed at Cognac in 1941. *Meyer*

Chapter 6

The Abbeville Boys: 1942

The winter lull in the fighting along the Channel was broken on 12 February by the famous Channel Dash, the escape of the German capital ships *Scharnhorst* and *Gneisenau* from Brest through the English Channel and the North Sea to Germany. Adolf Galland, the new General of the Fighter Arm, planned the fighter escort mission in Berlin and directed it from the JG 26 command post. His escort plan worked flawlessly. No British bomb or torpedo struck a German ship. JG 26 played a principal role in the operation, which was one of the greatest blows to British pride and prestige of the entire war.

In March the RAF resumed its light day bombing raids across the Channel. JG 26 was now equipped entirely with FW 190A-1s and FW 190A-2s; both models were vastly superior to the Spitfire V. JG 26, assisted by JG 2, easily dominated the skies over the Channel narrows. German aerial victories that spring and summer

A picture postcard sent by the non-commissioned JG 26 pilots in POW camp in Canada to the Geschwader's commissioned pilots in another Canadian camp. Top row, from left: Uffz. Werner Schammert, Obfw. Franz Lueders, Uffz. Martin Schroepfer, Fw. Gerhard Herzog, Uffz. Heinz Bock, Uffz. Horst Liebeck, Uffz. Horst Perez, Uffz. Ernst Braun, Uffz. Oswald Fischer, Fw. Walter Braun. Bottom row, from left: Obfw. Gerhard Grzymalla, Fw. Martin Klar, Fw. Karl Straub, Obfw. Otto Jaros, Obfw. Robert Schiffbauer, Obfw. Josef Gaertner, Uffz. Konrad von Jutrzenka, Fw. Arnold Kuepper, Obfw. Konrad Jaeckel—a near-complete roster of enlisted pilots taken prisoner through 1942. *Buerschgens*

Adolf Galland's younger brothers, Oblt. Wilhelm-Ferdinand "Wutz" (KIA 17 Aug 43) and Lt. Paul (KIA 31 Oct 42), photographed on the Kanalfront in 1942. Both were killed in combat while in JG 26. This "pass-along" copy print is unfortunately of poor quality. *Strasen via Roba*

Adolf Galland in a favorite service portrait from 1942—at age thirty, the Wehrmacht's youngest general. *Galland*

exceeded their losses by a ratio of about four to one. The Second Gruppe under Hptm. Joachim Muencheberg gained a reputation as an especially aggressive, well-led unit. Based at Abbeville-Drucat for the entire year, the Gruppe was nicknamed the "Abbeville Boys" by the RAF pilots; this was later Americanized to "Abbeville Kids" and extended to the whole Geschwader.

Two specialized Staffeln were formed and added to the strength of the Geschwader. The first, 10(Jabo)/JG 26, was a fighter-bomber Staffel equipped initially with Bf 109F-4/Bs, which carried a single 250kg bomb. In June it received FW 190A-3/U3s, which could carry one 500kg and four 50kg bombs. The Staffel operated independently from St. Omer-Wizernes; its aircraft flew small-scale hit-and-run raids to southern England, harrying the British defenses but doing negligible damage. The second new Staffel was 11(Hoehen)/JG 26, which was administered by the First Gruppe; it was equipped with the Bf 109G-1 and specialized in high-altitude combat. In November it was sent to North Africa, where it suffered such crippling casualties that it was soon disbanded.

The large-scale RAF daylight attacks across the Channel came to an end with the raid on Dieppe on 19 August, which cost the RAF 106 aircraft for a German loss of forty-eight fighters and bombers. JG 26 claimed forty victories and lost six pilots.

The B-17 and B-24 heavy bombers of the American Eighth Air Force began arriving in England at midyear. Their buildup was slow, and in 1942 American raids were confined to the coastal region, within range of their Spitfire escort. The Germans could not afford to ignore these attacks, which had a potential for damage much greater than those of the RAF light bombers, but they were stymied at first by the heavy defensive armament and close formations of the American bombers. Late 1942 was thus a time of testing for both sides. With the Spitfire IX the RAF fighter force attained qualitative parity with the German fighter forces on the Channel, which at year's end were equipped entirely with the FW 190A-4.

Photographic coverage of this period is more complete than for any other period in the Geschwader's history. An attempt has been made to document the daily activities on some of the unit's airfields, especially Abbeville-Drucat, Wevelghem, and Moorsele. The personal photograph collection of Peter Crump, a pilot in JG 26 and III/JG 54 from 1942 to 1945, has been especially valuable.

Maj. Gerhard Schoepfel in a Stab FW 190A-2 at Audembert in early 1942. The "S" identifies the aircraft as that of his adjutant, Oblt. Wilfried Sieling. *Bundesarchiv*

Hptm. Wilhelm Gaeth's Geschwaderstab FW 190A-2. *Meyer*

Uffz. Oswald Fischer's 10th (Jabo) Staffel Bf 109F-4/B fighter-bomber, photographed after it crash-landed at Beachy Head, England, on 20 May 1942. *Payne*

Maj. Schoepfel and his immaculate FW 190A-2 return to St. Omer from a mission. *Bundesarchiv*

The Channel Dash—JG 26 FW 190s patrol the course of the German fleet up the English Channel on 12 February. *Bundesarchiv*

An early FW 190A-4 of the Geschwaderstab, W.Nr. 5613, at St. Omer. It was probably assigned on paper to the technical officer, Fliegerstabsingenieur Ernst Battmer, who did not fly combat missions. *Meyer*

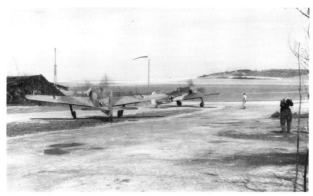

Geschwaderstab FW 190A-2s taxi out for a mission from Audembert in early 1942. Oblt. Sieling was killed in "He" on 30 April. *Bundesarchiv*

Hptm. Johannes Seifert, First Gruppe Kommandeur, gets the assistance of the Gruppe mascot in removing his belt of flare cartridges. Seifert was a prewar member of the First Gruppe who served quietly as 3rd Staffel Kapitaen throughout 1940 and became Kommandeur in July 1941. He later transferred to the Second Gruppe and was killed on 25 November 1943 in a collision with an American 55th Fighter Group P-38. *Meyer*

Lt. Bruno Hegenauer, a favorite wingman of both Obstlt. Galland and Maj. Schoepfel. Hegenauer flew to North Africa in November with 11/JG 26, was transferred to JG 53, and was killed attempting to evacuate Tunisia in May 1943. *Genth*

A 1st Staffel FW 190A-3 takes off from St. Omer. Note the absence of the outer wing guns; the Geschwader frequently removed them to improve maneuverability. *Meyer*

First Gruppe FW 190A-4s at St. Omer in 1942 or 1943. *Genth*

1st Staffel ground crewman Uffz. Hans Backhaus helps ready his Kapitaen, Oblt. Josef Haiboeck, for takeoff from St. Omer-Arques. *Meyer*

The 3rd Staffel's Uffz. Herbert Bremer parks his FW 190A-4 "Yellow 5" after scoring his first victory. Photographed in St. Omer-Ft. Rouge, 11 October. *Bundesarchiv*

Fw. Heinrich "Jan" Schild of the 2nd Staffel sits on his "Black 6" at St. Omer in 1942. Schild served in the Geschwader from 1942 to V-E Day. *Schild*

Uffz. Bremer watches while his first victory tab is painted on his mud-spattered rudder. He was killed in this aircraft three months later. *Bundesarchiv*

The Second Gruppe pilots were quartered in this large chateau outside Abbeville. *Crump*

A No. 303 Sqd. (Polish) Spitfire V is dismantled for salvage. It was downed near St. Omer on 4 April by First Gruppe Focke-Wulfs. *Bundesarchiv*

Obfw. Waldemar Soeffing, a long-serving pilot in the First Gruppe, in his 1st Staffel FW 190A. *Soeffing via Schmidt*

Mealtime at an Abbeville 2cm flak position. *Genth*

The Second Gruppe's Bf 108 Taifun courier aircraft, often piloted by Joachim Muencheberg. *Reimers via Ebert*

An Abbeville 2cm flak position. *Naumann via Roba*

The First Gruppe takes off from St. Omer on a 1942 mission. *Bundesarchiv*

An Abbeville hangar after suffering what was reported as light damage during an attack by ten Royal Air Force Bostons in the summer of 1942. *Crump*

Hptm. Egon Mayer of JG 2 (center) visits the Second Gruppe at Abbeville; he is standing between Hptm. Muencheberg and Oblt. Kurt Ebersberger. Mayer is generally credited with originating the most effective tactic against American bomber formations—the head-on attack. *Genth*

The Abbeville reservoir made an attractive swimming pool for the Second Gruppe in the summer of 1942, despite a forbidding list of restrictions. *Crump*

The Abbeville landing signals Gefreiter on a lazy summer afternoon. *Bundesarchiv*

A typical 1942 Abbeville scene—extinguishing a fire in a BMW 801 engine. The victim is a 5th Staffel FW 190A-3. *Meyer*

This No. 222 Sqd. (RAF) Spitfire Mk. VB came to rest on the bank of the Somme Estuary on 30 April, after a large-scale combat with the First and Second Gruppen. *Crump*

Hptm. Kurt Ebersberger and his 4th Staffel in mid-1942. From left: Obfw. Willi Roth, Lt. Ernst Janda (KIA 3 Sep 43), Fhr. Waldemar Radener, Uffz. Gerhard Birke (KIFA 17 May 43), Hptm. Ebersberger (KIA 24 Oct 43), Fw. Adolf "Addi" Glunz. *Genth*

An Abbeville signals detachment. *Bundesarchiv*

The Abbeville firefighting crew on duty—waiting for the next engine fire. *Bundesarchiv*

A 4th Staffel FW 190A-3 is serviced by the Staffel armorers at Abbeville. *Bundesarchiv*

Addi Glunz's luck never deserted him—this time he returned uninjured to Abbeville with shell holes in the wings of his FW 190. *Glunz*

"Black 8," a 5th Staffel FW 190A-3; Oblt. Wutz Galland's regular aircraft in mid-1942, photographed at Abbeville. *Crump*

"Black 3," a 5th Staffel FW 190A-3, W.Nr. 538; Obfw. Gerhardt was killed in this aircraft off Dieppe on 19 August. *Crump*

Obfw. Werner Gerhardt (with bouquet) is congratulated for his 100th mission with several rounds of drinks; his Staffelkapitaen, Oblt. Wutz Galland, is the man wearing white shorts. Photographed at Abbeville, mid-1942. *Crump*

"Black 2," the 5th Staffel FW 190A-3 in which Uffz. Peter Crump shot down his first enemy aircraft, a Spitfire, on 27 August. *Crump*

Soccer was a popular sport that could be played during brief breaks in the routine—this is the 6th Staffel at Abbeville. *Meyer*

The 5th Staffel's Obfw. Heinz Bierwirth watches his FW 190A-3 receive its fourth victory bar on 5 June 1942. Bierwirth was killed over England on 27 November. *Crump*

The 6th Staffel whiles away the hours at readiness at Abbeville with lectures. *Meyer*

"Brown 6," a 6th Staffel FW 190A-3, is towed to the Abbeville engine shop. *Bundesarchiv*

The entire Third Gruppe Stab flight is lined up outside the Gruppe's command post at Wevelghem in mid-1942. Hptm.

Josef Priller's is the lead FW 190A-2. Note the distinctive chevron and bar markings on each aircraft. *Priller*

Hptm. Priller and Fw. Gruenlinger at Wevelghem, next to one of Priller's FW 190A-2s, W.Nr. 0552. The aircraft's seventy-seven victory bars date the photograph between 29 August and 9 October. Gruenlinger was Priller's wingman in the Third Gruppe and later on the Geschwaderstab. Gruenlinger was killed by Spitfires on 4 September 1943, one day after being named leader of the 10th Staffel. *Priller*

Hptm. Priller keeps an eye on his command from a Wevelghem balcony. The caption on the original photograph, in Priller's handwriting, reads, "A bomb crater near my aircraft is filled in quickly. Everything must be in shape for a rapid takeoff!" *Priller*

FW 190A-3 W.Nr. 152 shows the effects of a bad landing after its delivery flight to Wevelghem in mid-1942. *Schmidt via Roba*

"In memory of the war"—the specific incident prompting the sign is not known. Hptm. Priller (center, on lap) is surrounded by his Staffelkapitaene and other Third Gruppe pilots. Second from left is Oblt. Karl Borris (8th Staffel); next, Oblt. Guenther Kelch (KIFA 31 Jul 43); 2nd from right, Oblt. Klaus Mietusch (7th Staffel); far right, Oblt. Kurt Ruppert (9th Staffel). *Vanoverbeke*

FW 190A-2s of the Third Gruppe stand ready for takeoff from Wevelghem. The nearest aircraft is that of Fw. Walter Gruenlinger (KIA 4 Sep 43); in the middle, a Gruppe staff aircraft; behind, a wingman's aircraft from the 7th Staffel. *Cranston*

When Fw. Gruenlinger inherited his Kommandeur's FW 190A-2 in April, Priller's *Jutta* was renamed *Rata*. Photographed at Wevelghem, August 1942. *Bundesarchiv*

Fw. Walter Gruenlinger. *Genth*

The 7th Staffel poses for a photograph while at readiness at Wevelghem in 1942. From left: Uffz. Hans Pritze (KIA 7 July 43), unknown, unknown, Oblt. Klaus Mietusch (KIA 17 Sep 44), Hptm. Guenther Kelch (KIFA 31 July 43), Uffz. Guenther Patzke (KIA 21 Sep 44), Uffz. Woege, Fw. Heinz Kemethmueller, unknown, unknown, Fw. Erich Jauer (POW 18 June 43), unknown. At the time Mietusch was the only pilot from the previous year's Mediterranean tour who was still with the Staffel. *Meyer*

Oblt. Mietusch, photographed beside the tail of his 7th Staffel FW 190A-3 in August. *Bundesarchiv*

Hptm. Priller poses in a tracked carrier at Wevelghem. *Schmidt*

The Adamsonstaffel's pet raven Jakob demonstrates one of his bad habits—playing with matches. *Schmidt*

Pilots of the 8th Staffel, photographed at Wevelghem in early 1942. From left: Uffz. Heinrich Waelter (KIA 28 Jan 43), Fw. Johann Edmann (KIA 21 Mar 44), Obfw. Max Martin, Fw. Wilhelm Latka (KIA 3 Nov 43), Fw. Robert Hager (KIA 13 Aug 44), Obfw. Willi Kalitzki (KIFA 29 Apr 44), and Obfw. Hans Heitmann. Seated: Oblt. Hans Geburtig (POW 30 Jul 42). *Bauerhenne*

Eighth Staffel ground crewman Uffz. Gottfried Schmidt and his FW 190A-2 "Black 2," photographed at Coquelles on the day of the Channel Dash—12 February 1942. *Schmidt*

Eighth Staffel FW 190A-3s at Wevelghem in late 1942. *Meyer*

The 8th Staffel's Fw. Robert Hager, photographed with Staffelhund Franz—probably at Wevelghem in 1942. *Schmidt*

Fw. Paul Thuilot polishes "Black 1," the aircraft of the 8th Staffel Kapitaen, Oblt. Karl Borris—Wevelghem, mid-1942. *Schmidt via Roba*

The Hollenhund emblem flew in front of the 9th Staffel's command post long after it disappeared from the Staffel's aircraft. Photographed in Moorsele, Belgium, 1942. *Vanoverbeke*

The 8th Staffel's Oblt. Kurt Kranefeld flies over the Belgian countryside in his "Black 11." Kranefeld drowned in a boating accident on 26 April 1944, while at a Cazaux rest camp. *Meyer*

A 9th Staffel FW 190A-3, having suffered a headstand, is stabilized prior to being righted. *Vanoverbeke*

The 9th Staffel's Lt. Otto "Stotto" Stammberger in a Belgian salvage yard. He is standing beside the vertical tail of Lt. Francis Chorak's American 92nd Bomber Group B-17E. The airplane was shot down by JG 26 on the 9 October Lille raid. *Abendroth*

A 9th Staffel FW 190A banks for the cameraman near Moorsele in August 1942. *Vanoverbeke*

Oblt. Ruppert confers with Hptm. Kelch and Lt. Stamm-berger beside his FW 190A-3. The yellow 27 paint of the identity codes photographs much lighter than the yellow 04 paint of the rudder. Photographed at Moorsele in August 1942. *Vanoverbeke*

The 9th Staffel's "Yellow 6" makes a slow circuit of Moorse-le in August, gear and flaps extended, for the benefit of the photographer. *Bundesarchiv*

The 9th Staffel's Moorsele base as seen from the air in August 1942; the unit's Hollenhund flag can be recognized. *Bundesarchiv*

Oblt. Kurt Ruppert, the long-time Kapitaen of the 9th Staffel, is given the "deutsche Gruss" (German salute) by two of his pilots, Lts. Guenther Kelch and Otto Stammberger, after a successful mission over the Dieppe beachhead. Ruppert downed three Spitfires this day. Photographed at Moorsele, 19 August. *Vanoverbeke*

The 9th Staffel's Uffz. Alfred Niese (KIA 25 Jun 43) points out the victory tally on Oblt. Ruppert's "Yellow 13" to Fw. Melchior Kestel (also KIA 25 Jun 43). Photographed at Moorsele, late 1942. *Vanoverbeke*

Fw. Kraft's "Yellow 11" forms the backdrop for a lecture on the Focke-Wulf fighter's electrical equipment at Moorsele, 1942. *Vanoverbeke*

Another view of the 9th Staffel's base at Moorsele. *Bundesarchiv*

Oblt. Ruppert exits "Yellow 13" at Moorsele. Ruppert was
killed on 13 June 1943, when his parachute harness failed
after his aircraft had been hit by B-17 fire. *Meyer*

Chapter 7

Germany Loses The Air War: January 1943–May 1944

On 10 January 1943, Maj. Schoepfel was succeeded as Kommodore by Maj. Josef "Pips" Priller, the popular Kommandeur of the Third Gruppe. The Jabo effort peaked with a day raid on London on 20 January that cost the Geschwader eight pilots. The 10th Staffel (Jabo) left the Geschwader soon afterward, joining a specialized Schnellkampfgeschwader (fast bomber wing). Other winter activity centered around the planned transfer of JG 26 to the Eastern Front, where it was to trade places with JG 54. Maj. Johannes Seifert's First Gruppe and Hptm. Klaus Mietusch's 7th Staffel left for northern Russia in late January, while III/JG 54 and 4/JG 54 came west. The 4th Staffel of JG 54 was subordinated to III/JG 26, while III/JG 54 operated independently from bases in northern Germany. The units of JG 26 on the Eastern Front compiled an excellent record, but were ordered to return to the Channel front in June to counter the growing strength of the American bomber attacks. The move of the rest of the Geschwader to the Eastern Front was canceled. Unfortunately, no publishable photographs of the First Gruppe or the 7th Staffel on the Eastern Front could be located for this book.

During the first half of 1943, the mission of the part of the Geschwader remaining in the west was to oppose the American heavy bombers and their P-47 and Spitfire escort. The preferred German method of attack on the bombers was from the front of the formation—from "twelve o'clock high." The Third Gruppe saw their FW 190As replaced with Bf 109Gs; the Luftwaffe High Command felt that the excellent high-altitude performance of these new Messerschmitt fighters made them a logical choice to equip the units in the west. The First and Second Gruppen kept their Focke-Wulfs. In 1943 the standard variant of the latter was the FW 190A-6, which carried a very effective armament of two light machine guns and four 20mm machine cannons. FW 190A-7s and FW 190A-8s arrived in 1944; in these models heavy machine guns replaced the two light ones,

giving them the heaviest weight of fire of any standard single-engined fighter of the war. In early 1943 three new Staffeln were added to JG 26, the 10th, 11th, and 12th, and the establishment strength of each of the Geschwader's Staffeln was increased from twelve to sixteen aircraft. After the four Staffeln in Russia returned, the Geschwader underwent a reorganization; seven of

Maj. Josef Priller in an FW 190A-5 with an unusual set of markings, the chevron-triangle of a Gruppenkommandeur and the pointed horizontal bar of the JG 26 Geschwader Stab. Photographed at Lille-Vendeville, spring 1943. *Meyer*

the unit's twelve Staffeln were assigned new numbers, and one, the Adamsonstaffel, moved to a different Gruppe. Establishment strength was now 208 aircraft; however, true operational strength averaged about half this figure.

By mid-1943 the American Eighth Air Force was regularly attacking targets in the interior of the continent, and the aerial defenses of Germany proper had to be bolstered with newly formed fighter units and experienced units withdrawn from the Mediterranean and Eastern Fronts. JG 26 and the other Jagdgeschwader in France and the Low Countries had the tasks of breaking up the bomber formations for the benefit of the units in Germany and of downing damaged bombers on their return trip. As the American escorts grew in strength and experience, it became more and more difficult for the forward German units to intercept the bombers without being in turn attacked by the American fighters. Attacking the escort early to force it away from the bomber stream, which would have been the most effective and logical mission for the forward units, was ex-

pressly forbidden by Goering. JG 26's casualty list began to grow.

The short range of the American P-47s, which forced them to turn back at the German border, gave the Luftwaffe fighter units based in Germany an advantage. Unescorted bomber formations proved very vulnerable to rocket-firing twin-engined fighters and specially armed and armored FW 190s. One of the greatest victories of the German day defenses was won on 17 August 1943 against the Schweinfurt-Regensburg raid; sixty B-17s were shot down out of 376 dispatched. Most were lost to the German home defenses, but the forward units did well also; JG 26 claimed seventeen B-17s, one Spitfire, one Typhoon, and one P-47 destroyed, for the loss of five of its own pilots killed and five wounded. The German success was duplicated two months later, on the second Schweinfurt raid, which cost the Americans another sixty B-17s.

Combat ebbed during the typically bad weather of the north European winter, but in early 1944, when the Americans next attempted to bomb central Germany,

Maj. Priller, his BMW automobile, and his BMW engine-equipped FW 190A-5, in a posed "movie star shot" at Lille-Vendeville, May-June 1943. *Bundesarchiv*

Maj. Priller (left) in a tactical command post. In all probability this photograph was taken while Priller was serving as interim Jafue at St. Pol in mid-1943. *Bundesarchiv*

Maj. Priller in flight in FW 190A-5 W.Nr. 7298, his regular aircraft during May and June 1943. *Bundesarchiv*

their bombers were escorted all the way to their targets by long-ranged P-51s and P-38s. The tide of the air war quickly turned in favor of the Allies. By the end of "Big Week," the name the Americans gave to six successive days of maximum-strength raids in late February, the Jagdwaffe was reduced to using hit-and-run tactics against the overwhelming strength of the bombers and escort. In the absence of any viable options, the mission of JG 26 and the other forward-based units remained the same, but their effectiveness grew less and less. Between 1 January and 5 June 1944, JG 26 lost 106 pilots, which was 140 percent of the average number of pilots available for duty with the Geschwader.

The majority of the photographs illustrating this chapter were taken in 1943, at the high point of the Luftwaffe's successes against the Eighth Air Force. The Geschwader's aircraft are typically shown parked in the open, clear evidence of Germany's belief in its own dominance of the skies over the Channel front.

Josef Priller and Bimbo, a French colonial soldier who was not repatriated after the 1940 campaign, but stayed in France to serve the Luftwaffe as an orderly. Photographed at Lille-Vendeville, mid-1943. *Bundesarchiv*

Obstlt. Priller beside his FW 190A-6, W.Nr. 530120. The right side of the fin carried only a partial Werke Nummer, while the left side displayed the complete number. Photographed at Lille-Nord, winter 1943–44. *Bundesarchiv*

Armorers load WGr. 21 rockets on an FW 190A-8/R6 of the JG 26 Stab. The white spiral on the (assumed) green spinner was non-standard for the period. Photographed at Lille-Vendeville, May 1944. *Bundesarchiv*

A less well-known photo from the series; this one shows the JG 26 Stab markings well. *Bundesarchiv*

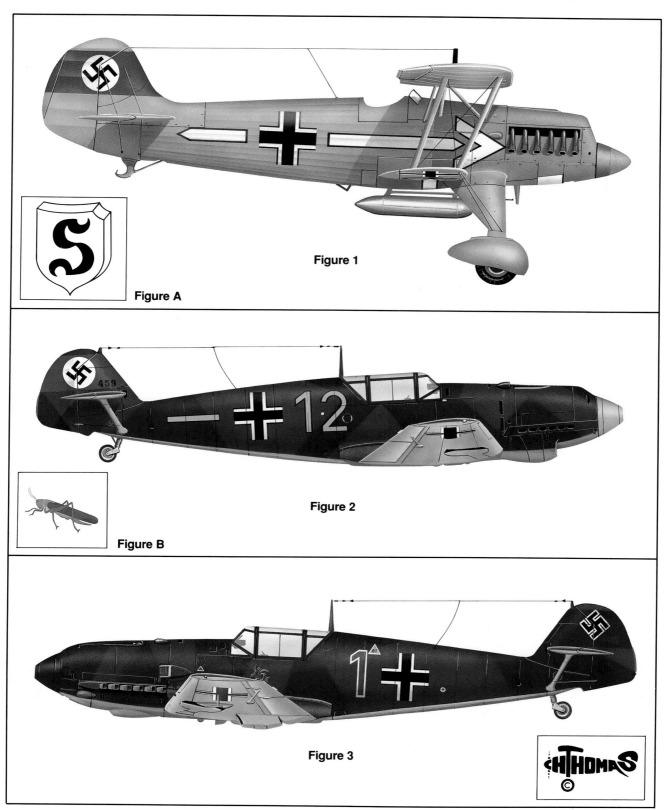

Figure A

Figure 1

Figure B

Figure 2

Figure 3

Figure 1: He 51B of Hptm. Oskar Dinort, I/JG 234's first Kommandeur—Cologne, early 1937. Figure 2: Bf 109B of 6/JG 234—Duesseldorf, early 1938. Figure 3: Bf 109E-1 of Hptm. Walter Kienitz, 2nd Staffel Kapitaen—Sylt, early 1939. Figure A: Geschwader emblem. Figure B: 1st Staffel emblem.

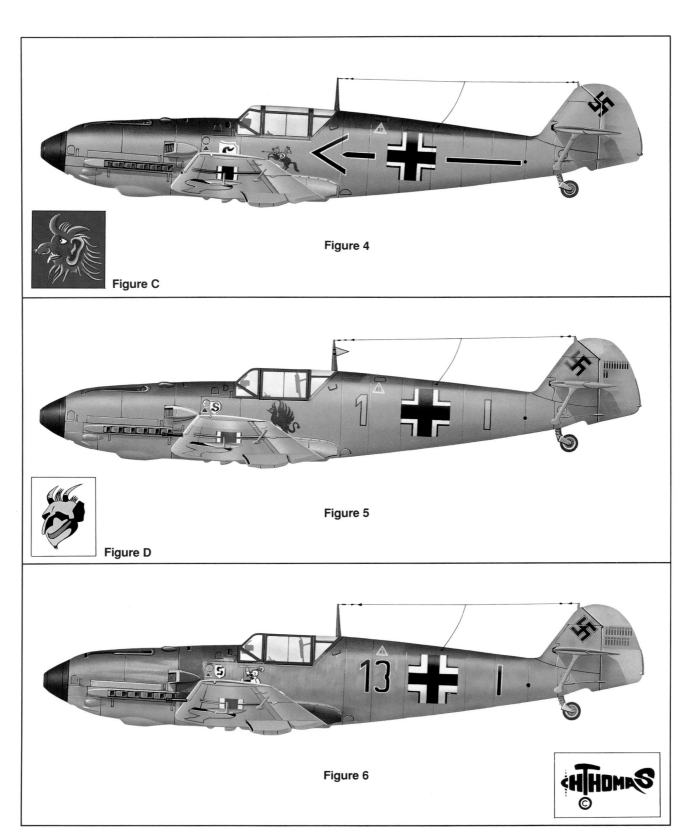

Figure 4

Figure C

Figure 5

Figure D

Figure 6

Figure 4: Bf 109E-1 of Maj. Hans-Hugo Witt, Geschwader Kommodore, early 1940. Figure 5: Bf 109E-4 of Oblt. Gerhard Schoepfel, 9th Staffel Kapitaen, mid-August 1940. Figure 6: Bf 109E-4/N of Oblt. Micky Sprick, 8th Staffel Kapitaen, late September 1940. Figure C: 2nd Staffel emblem, early form. Figure D: 2nd Staffel emblem, late form.

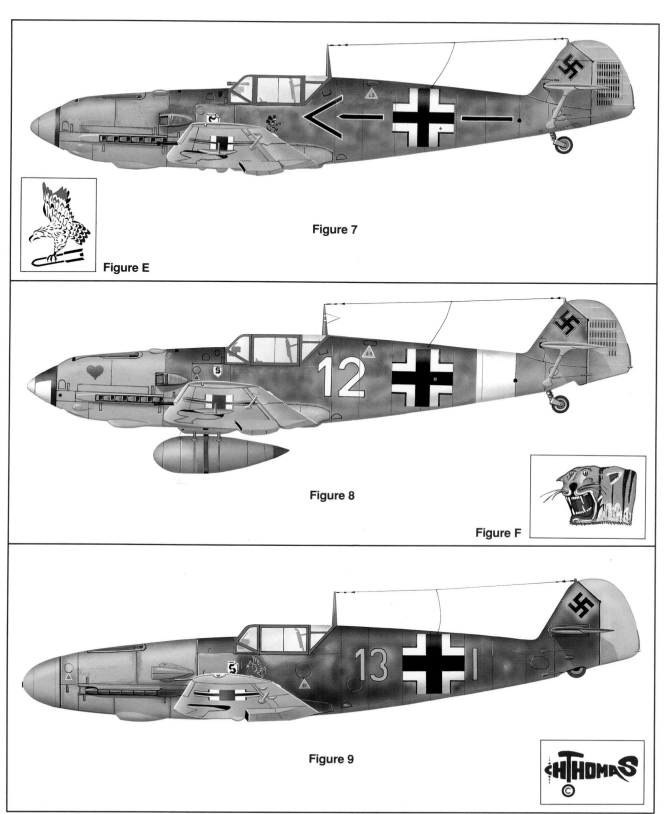

Figure 7

Figure E

Figure 8

Figure F

Figure 9

Figure 7: Bf 109E-4/N of Obstlt. Adolf Galland, Geschwader Kommodore, December 1940. Figure 8: Bf 109E-7 of Oblt. Joachim Muencheberg, 7th Staffel Kapitaen, March 1941.

Figure 9: Bf 109F-2 of the 9th Staffel, spring 1941. Figure E: 3rd Staffel emblem (probably unofficial). Figure F: 4th Staffel emblem.

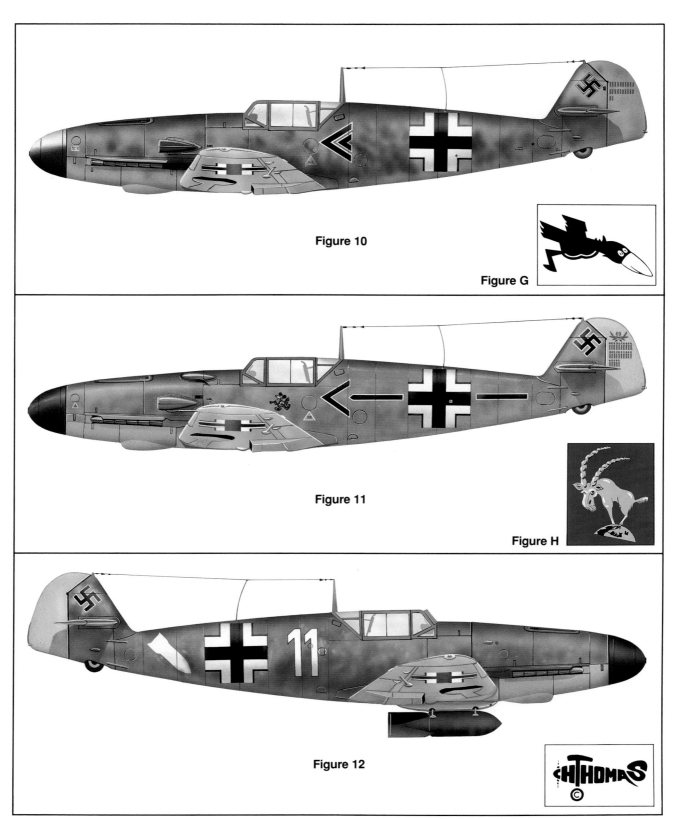

Figure 10

Figure G

Figure 11

Figure H

Figure 12

Figure 10: Bf 109F-2 of Hptm. Rolf Pingel, First Gruppe Kommandeur, 10 July 1941. Figure 11: Bf 109F-2/U of Obstlt. Adolf Galland, Geschwader Kommodore, 5 December 1941. Figure 12: Bf 109F-4/B of Uffz. Oswald Fischer, 10th (Jabo) Staffel, 20 May 1942. Figure G: 5th Staffel emblem. Figure H: 6th Staffel emblem.

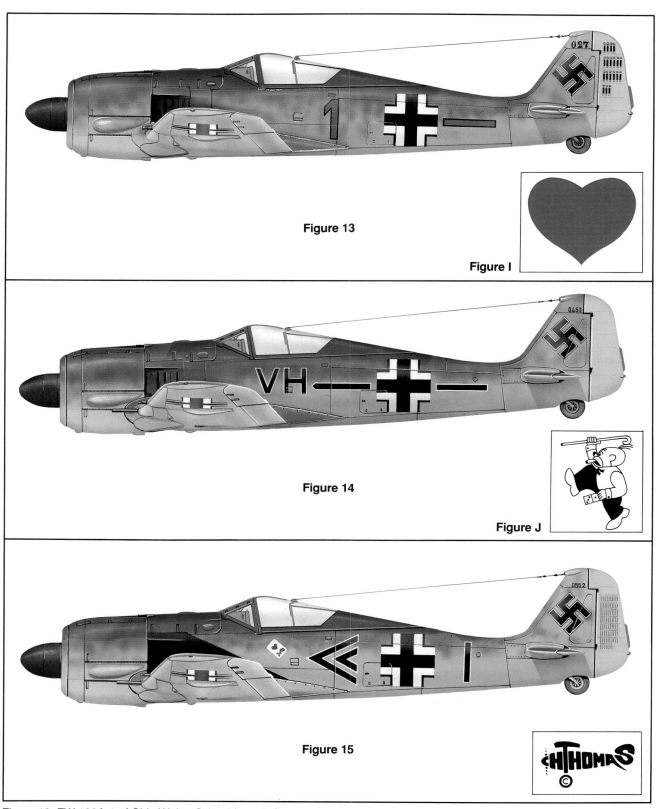

Figure 13

Figure I

Figure 14

Figure J

Figure 15

Figure 13: FW 190A-1 of Oblt. Walter Schneider, 6th Staffel Kapitaen, September 1941. Figure 14: FW 190A-2 of Oblt. Viktor Hilgendorff, Geschwader Stab, early 1942. Figure 15: FW 190A-3 of Hptm. Josef Priller, Third Gruppe Kommandeur, September 1942. Figure I: 7th Staffel emblem. Figure J: 8th Staffel emblem.

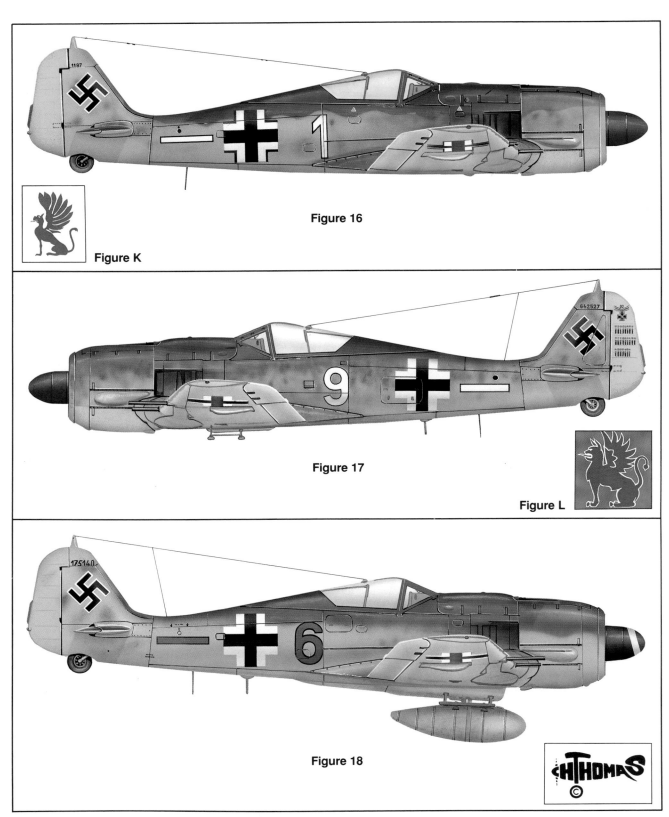

Figure K

Figure 16

Figure 17

Figure L

Figure 18

Figure 16: FW 190A-5 of Oblt. Otto Stammberger, 4th Staffel Kapitaen—Vitry-en-Artois, early 1943. Figure 17: FW 190A-7 of Obfw. Adolf Glunz, 5th Staffel—Cambrai, February 1944. Figure 18: FW 190A-8 of the 7th Staffel—Melsbroek, 3 September 1944. Figure K: 9th Staffel emblem, early form. Figure L: 9th Staffel emblem, late form.

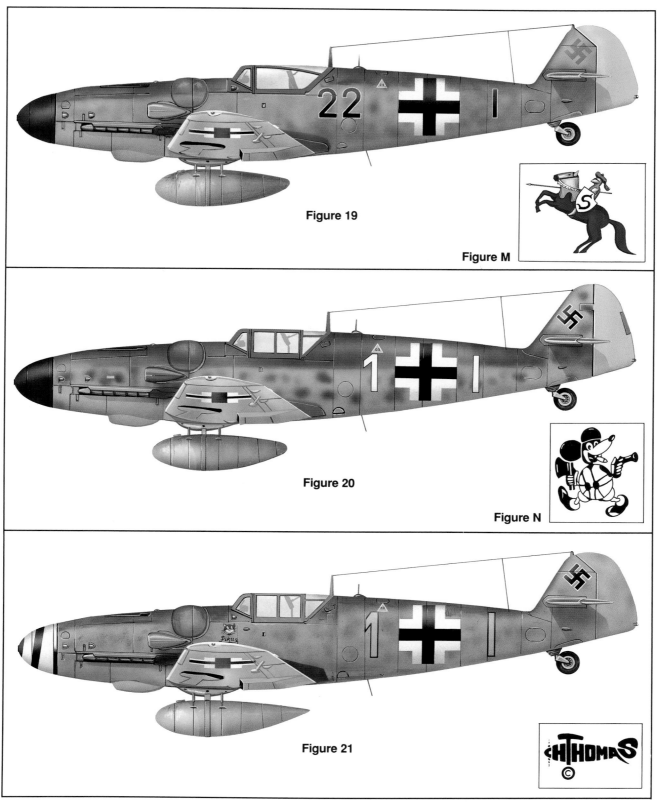

Figure 19

Figure M

Figure 20

Figure N

Figure 21

Figure 19: Bf 109G-6 of Maj. Klaus Mietusch, Third Gruppe Kommandeur—Lille, March or April 1944. Figure 20: Bf 109G-6 of the 9th Staffel—Lille, March or April 1944.

Figure 21: Bf 109G-6 of Uffz. Heinz Gehrke, 11th Staffel—Villacoublay, July 1944. Figure M: Geschwader Stab emblem. Figure N: Adolf Galland's personal emblem.

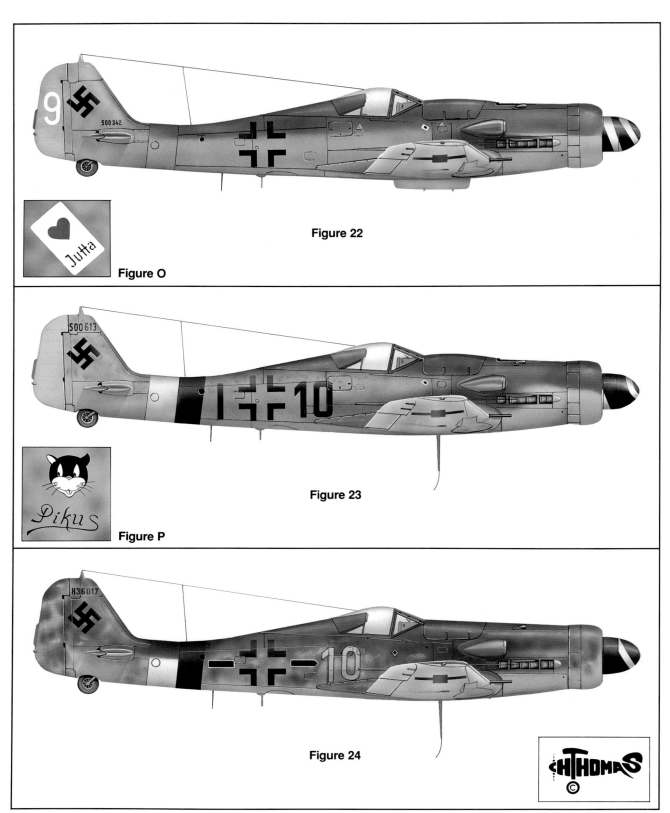

Figure 22

Figure O

Figure 23

Figure P

Figure 24

Figure 22: FW 190D-9 flown by the Second Gruppe in conversion training—Reinsehlen, November 1944. Figure 23: FW 190D-9 of the 10th Staffel—Celle, March 1945. Figure 24: FW 190D-13 of Maj. Franz Goetz, Geschwader Kommodore—Flensburg, May 1945. Figure O: Josef Priller's personal emblem. Figure P: Heinz Gehrke's personal emblem.

The engine of a Second Gruppe FW 190A-6 Jabo is run up for the benefit of Feldmarschall Rommel, in a demonstration of the Luftwaffe's planned response to the forthcoming Al-lied invasion. Photographed at Lille-Vendeville, May or early June 1944. *Bundesarchiv*

Feldmarschall Rommel inspects Obstlt. Priller's regular FW 190A-6, W.Nr. 530120, under the cameras at Lille-Vendeville, May or early June 1944. *Bundesarchiv*

An FW 190A-4/U3 of 10(Jabo)/JG 26 taxies out with a 500kg bomb. Photographed at St. Omer-Wizernes, 8 January 1943. *Bundesarchiv*

Karl Borris, seen here as an Oberleutnant in 1942. The only prewar JG 26 pilot still flying with the Geschwader on V-E Day, Maj. Borris commanded the First Gruppe for almost two full years. *Genth*

Lt. Artur Beese, a prewar member of the Geschwader and Kapitaen of the 1st Staffel from mid-1943 until he was killed by a P-47 on 6 February 1944. *Beese via Roba*

An FW 190A-5/U3 fighter-bomber of 10(Jabo)/JG 54, which 10(Jabo)/JG 26 became in February 1943. *Bundesarchiv*

The 3rd Staffel's Fw. Karl Willius. Promoted to Oberleutnant and given command of the 2nd Staffel, Willius was shot down and killed by American 361st Fighter Group P-47s on 8 April 1944, after scoring his forty-eighth victory. He received his Knight's Cross posthumously. *Bundesarchiv via Charlier*

The 2nd Staffel's Obfw. Emil Babenz. A highly experienced pilot with twenty-four air victories, Babenz was killed on 8 April 1944 in the same combat that claimed the life of his Kapitaen, Karl Willius. *Bundesarchiv via Charlier*

Eighth Staffel pilots at Lille-Vendeville in mid-1943. The Staffel had separated from the Third Gruppe at this time and was flying as Maj. Priller's Fuehrungsstaffel (lead squadron). From left: Oblt. Kurt Kranefeld (drowned 28 Apr 44), Uffz. Horst-Guenther Schoehl, Uffz. Norbert Holtz, unknown, Obfw. Johann Edmann (KIA 21 Mar 44), Fw. Kurt Schmidtke (KIA 7 Jul 44). *Wiegand via Roba*

An air battle over Wevelghem in January 1943. This photo was taken by Gerd Wiegand, a serious student of air combat, who made the notations on the print. *Wiegand via Mombeek*

"Black 12," the FW 190A of Uffz. Norbert Holtz, after a slight accident at Wevelghem in the late summer of 1943. The engine failed on the approach; Holtz stalled the aircraft, which cartwheeled and landed on its gear. Holtz was unhurt, but was demoted to Obergefreiter shortly thereafter. *Wiegand via Roba*

Four 8th Staffel non-commissioned pilots in late summer 1943. From left: Fw. Kurt Schmidtke, Fw. Erich Schwarz, Uffz. Gerd Wiegand, Uffz. Horst-Guenther Schoehl. *Niesmak*

The Adamsonstaffel at Wevelghem. The Staffel retained its strong unit identity through several redesignations. Formerly the Third Gruppe's 8th Staffel, it joined the First Gruppe as its 4th Staffel on 1 October 1943. From left: Uffz. Wiegand, Lt. Helmut Menge, Oblt. Wolfgang Neu, Fw. Schmidtke, Ogfr. Holtz, Fw. Hager, Fw. Schwarz, unknown, Uffz. Paul Erpenbach, unknown. *Wiegand via Mombeek*

Fw. Kurt Schmidtke of the newly redesignated 4th Staffel in his "Blue 5" at Wevelghem in early 1944. Schmidtke was killed by a P-51 on 7 July 1944, on the Invasion Front. *Schmidt via Roba*

An angled drop tank trolley devised by Fw. Wiegand while at Wevelghem in early 1944. It permitted full tanks to be mounted and removed from the aircraft quickly. Uffz. Ruestenkamp is apparently smoking a cigarette while the tank is filling. *Schmidt*

Hptm. Wolfgang Neu, successor to Hptm. Ebersberger as Kapitaen of the 4th Staffel, in his FW 190A-6. Neu was born on 11 September 1909 and was killed by bomber defensive fire on 22 April 1944. He was the oldest pilot in JG 26 at the time of his death. *Balloff via Eickhoff*

A Propaganda Company photographer receives last-minute instructions from the 4th Staffel's Ofhr. Wolfgang Rose (KIA 27 Jun 44) before being taken aloft at Wevelghem in early 1944. *Bundesarchiv*

"Blue 10," a 4th Staffel FW 190A-8, W.Nr. 730414, is taxied out by Ofhr. Rose for takeoff from Wevelghem with a pho-tographer in the baggage compartment. Lt. Helmut Menge was killed in this aircraft on 10 June 1944. *Bundesarchiv*

The photographer holds an underwing camera, for use when tagalong missions were too dangerous. It is marked, with German humor, "keine Bombe" (This is not a bomb). *Bundesarchiv*

Adamsonstaffel pilots take a break to pose for the Propaganda Company cameraman. From left: Ogfr. Norbert Holtz, Fw-Fhr. Gerd Wiegand, Ogfr. Heinz Wodarczyk (KIA 1 Jan 1945). Photographed at Wevelghem, early 1944. *Bundesarchiv*

Hptm. Wilhelm-Ferdinand Galland, Kommandeur of the Second Gruppe. The second Galland brother to die in the Geschwader, "Wutz" was killed on 17 August 1943 by American 56th Fighter Group P-47s escorting the Schweinfurt-Regensburg raiders. *Bundesarchiv*

The tail section of Lt. Clarence Fischer's 306th Bomber Group B-17, which was shot down by Hptm. Galland on 5 April 1943 and fell near Kappelle, Belgium. *Stammberger*

Hptm. Hans Naumann. A member of the Geschwader from 1938, Naumann commanded the 6th Staffel in 1943 and the Second Gruppe for the first half of 1944, and left JG 26 after being wounded in June. He was awarded the Knight's Cross late in the war, after scoring thirty-four western victories. *Meyer*

The funeral of Maj. Wilhelm-Ferdinand Galland. His parents are flanked by his brother Adolf, his Kommodore, Obstlt. Priller, and the Jagdfliegerfuehrer West, Genmaj. Max Ibel. *Stammberger via Roba*

Second Gruppe pilots walk to their planes. An FW 190A-7 is parked in the foreground. Photographed at Cambrai, February 1944. *Bundesarchiv*

Pilots of the 4th Staffel gather around their Kapitaen, Oblt. Stammberger. From left: unknown, Obfw. Adolf Glunz, unknown, Stammberger, Fw. Hermann Meyer (KIA 13 Mar 43), Lt. Guenther Bloemertz, Lt. Dietrich Kehl (KIA 25 Feb 44). Photographed at Vitry-en-Artois, early 1943. *Meyer*

Oblt. Helmut Hoppe, successor to Oblt. Stammberger as Kapitaen of the 4th Staffel, which became the 5th Staffel in the reorganization of 1 October 1943. Hoppe was shot down and killed by Spitfires while taking off from Epinoy on 1 December 1943. *Crump*

The rudder of Obfw. Glunz's FW 190A-5, W.Nr. 7321, showing thirty-nine victories. Photographed at Beauvais, 31 August 1943. *Mombeek*

Oblt. Otto Stammberger, Kapitaen of the 4th Staffel from 26 February 1943 until he was seriously wounded by No. 331 Sqd. (RNAF) Spitfires on 13 May 1943. *Bundesarchiv*

Adolf Glunz's spring 1943 "White 9," W.Nr. 0739, at Vitry-en-Artois, marked with twenty-nine victory bars. Otto Stammberger was shot down in this aircraft on 13 May. *Meyer*

Obfw. Glunz makes a "cavalier's dismount" from his FW 190A-7 "White 9," W.Nr. 642527, in February 1944. *Glunz*

Maj. Priller congratulates Obfw. Glunz on his newly award-ed Knight's Cross in August 1943. *Meyer*

Obfw. Glunz stands beside his FW 190A-7 after his best day as a fighter pilot—one P-47 and three B-17s shot down, and two B-17s driven from their formations. Photographed at Cambrai-Epinoy, 22 February 1944. *Glunz*

Oblt. Adolf Glunz's late-war service portrait. The amazing Addi Glunz was never shot down or injured while scoring seventy-two victories. He was Kapitaen of the 6th Staffel (the renumbered 5th) for twelve months in 1944–45. *Glunz*

5th Staffel pilots at Vitry-en-Artois in early 1943. From left: Lt. Paul Fritsch (KIA 6 Jul 43), Uffz. Erich Kleffner (KIA 20 Apr 43), Uffz. Peter Crump, Obfw. Wilhelm Freuwoerth, Uffz. Albert Meyer (KIA 3 Apr 43), Uffz. Heinrich Krieg (KIA 27 Aug 43), Uffz. Heinz Backeberg (KIA 14 May 1943). *Crump*

Oblt. Walter Matoni exits his FW 190A-7 "White 5" at Cambrai in February 1944. Matoni led the 5th Staffel (the renumbered 4th) for six months in 1944 before leaving JG 26 to take command of I/JG 11. *Bundesarchiv*

The 5th Staffel's Uffz. Crump and one of his "Black 10s," an FW 190A-4 photographed at Vitry-en-Artois, 1943. *Crump*

Peter Crump and his crew chief beside his FW 190A-4 "Black 10," W.Nr. 5658, at Vitry-en-Artois in early 1943. *Crump*

117

The 5th Staffel's Fw. Peter Crump, photographed at Vitry-en-Artois in mid-1943, his most successful period as a fighter pilot. *Crump*

The 5th Staffel's Waffenmeister (chief armorer) Wronczeks demonstrates a weapon he built around an MG 151 machine cannon that was salvaged from a crashed aircraft. It was meant to be a defense against low-flying aircraft. Photographed at Vitry-en-Artois, 1943. *Crump*

Four 5th Staffel pilots pose with FW 190A-4 "Black 11," W.Nr. 598. Obfw. Alfred Guenther landed this aircraft safely after being injured by Spitfires on 24 June 1943. Photographed at Vitry-en-Artois. *Crump*

Hptm. Hans Naumann, 6th Staffel Kapitaen, prepares to take off from Vitry-en-Artois in his FW 190A-6 on 26 July 1943. *Bundesarchiv*

Uffz. Heinz Gomann brought his FW 190A-5 "Black 22," W.Nr. 1243, back to base on 15 July 1943 after colliding with a Spitfire, which crashed. Gomann bailed out of this aircraft on 17 August 1943, after it was hit by P-47s escorting the Schweinfurt-Regensburg bomber force. *Crump*

A 5th Staffel ground crewman shows off FW 190A-4 "Black 5," W.Nr. 2379, at Vitry-en-Artois. Uffz. Heinrich Krieg was killed in this aircraft on 27 August 1943. *Crump*

Uffz. Heinz Gomann, a pilot in the Second Gruppe from 1942 until his transfer to jets in early 1945. *Crump*

Fw. Peter Crump and another of his "Black 10s," this one an FW 190A-6—Vitry-en-Artois, 1943. *Crump*

A No. 88 Sqd. (RAF) Boston III after its forced landing near Vendeville on 26 July 1943. Hptm. Naumann, the victorious pilot, is admiring his trophy. He and the surviving British crew met at a post-war reunion and remain correspondents. *Bundesarchiv*

The 6th Staffel forms up for takeoff, led by Hptm. Naumann in his "Brown 1." *Bundesarchiv*

"Brown 5," a 7th Staffel FW 190A-8, taxies out for takeoff in the spring of 1944 with a photographer in the baggage compartment. The fighter has the light-weight drop tank rack common in JG 26 during this period. *Bundesarchiv*

Hptm. Fritz Geisshardt. He transferred into the Geschwader from JG 77 to take over the Third Gruppe when Priller was promoted to Kommodore in January 1943. Geisshardt had won the Knight's Cross with Oak Leaves on the Eastern Front. *Roba*

The 7th Staffel's Obfw. Walter Meyer. A very successful pilot on the Channel front, Meyer died on 18 January 1943 from tuberculosis contracted in the hospital while recovering from injuries suffered in a ground collision on 11 October 1942. *Vanoverbeke*

The 9th Staffel's Obfw. Heinrich Humburg with a Bf 109G-4/R6, one of the first Bf 109 models to carry underwing 20mm cannons. *Genth*

A 12th Staffel Bf 109G-2 in mid-1943. *Genth*

The Third Gruppe celebrates its 500th victory of the war while based at Lille in mid-1943. Fw. Xaver Ellenrieder and Uffz. Gerd Wiegand are presented with flowers by a local French beauty. *Wiegand via Mombeek*

Oblt. Erwin Leykauf's 12th Staffel Bf 109G-6 after he attempted to take off during a carpet-bombing attack on Lille-Vendeville on 14 May 1943. Leykauf was uninjured. *Leykauf*

The 9th Staffel scrambles in its brand new Bf 109G-6s. The Staffel's yellow identity numbers and Gruppe bars are very light in hue, a characteristic also noticeable in photographs of the Staffel's FW 190s taken in 1942. Photographed at Wevelghem, April or May 1943. *Bundesarchiv*

The 9th Staffel's Bf 109G-6s scramble from Wevelghem in April or May 1943. *Bundesarchiv*

The 9th Staffel's Kapitaen, Hptm. Peter-Paul Steindl (KIFA 9 Jan 45), lectures Fw. Edgar Doerre (KIA 8 Sep 43) on tactics versus Spitfires. Photographed at Wevelghem, April-May 1943. *Bundesarchiv*

The funeral procession for Hptm. Geisshardt at Wevelghem. He died on 6 April 1943 of wounds received from B-17 gunners the previous day. *Vanoverbeke*

Hptm. Klaus Mietusch (left) and his adjutant, Lt. Ernst Todt, in the summer of 1943. Mietusch became Third Gruppe Kommandeur in July 1943 and served until his death in combat with an American 361st Fighter Group P-51on 17 September 1944. Todt was killed by Spitfires on 19 September 1943. *Genth*

The Bf 109G-6 of the 9th Staffel's Uffz. Robert Pautner under attack by Lt. Leroy Ista of the USAAF's 353rd Fighter Group near Gelsenkirchen on 5 November 1943. Pautner bailed out and survived, with wounds. *Roba*

A Third Gruppe Bf 109G undergoes maintenance in France in early 1944. *Genth*

125

Maj. Mietusch in one of the Third Gruppe Stab's Bf 109G-6s, "Black 20." Mietusch's Knight's Cross dates the photo as later than 26 March 1944. *Bundesarchiv*

An early example of a Bf 109G-6 with a tall vertical tail, which later became standard. The pilot of "White 1" is unknown; the Third Gruppe Staffelkapitaene all flew high-numbered aircraft. Photographed at Lille-Nord, March or April 1944. *Bundesarchiv*

A taxiing 11th Staffel Bf 109G-6, "Yellow 9," photographed as part of a series taken when the Third Gruppe landed at Lille-Nord for refueling during a transfer flight. The date is after 26 March 1944, and before (or as) the Gruppe left for southern Germany on 18 April. *Bundesarchiv*

Lt. Hans-Georg Dippel. Kapitaen of the 9th Staffel from August 1943, he was killed in a flying accident on 8 May 1944, after scoring nineteen air victories in 272 combat sorties. *Genth*

Hptm. Hermann Staiger. An exceptionally skilled formation leader, Staiger commanded the 12th Staffel and served as deputy commander of the First and Third Gruppen before transferring from the Geschwader at the end of July 1944. *Genth*

Hptm. Hans-Georg Dippel, 9th Staffel Kapitaen, taxies in Bf 109G-6 "White 17," the aircraft in which he was killed on 8 May. It is noteworthy that this aircraft does not have the Erla-Haube (clear canopy), which equipped most of the Third Gruppe's aircraft at this time. Photographed at Lille-Nord, March or April 1944. *Bundesarchiv*

A taxiing 9th Staffel Bf 109G-6. This airplane has an Erla-Haube, which markedly improved a pilot's vision from the Messerschmitt's cramped cockpit. Photographed at Lille-Nord, March or April 1944. *Bundesarchiv*

Lt. Karl-Heinz Kempf prepares to board his Bf 109G-6 at Lille-Nord in March or April 1944. Kempf was a very popular officer who won the Knight's Cross with JG 54 on the Eastern Front before joining JG 26 in late 1943. He was killed with the 2nd Staffel during a disastrous transfer flight on 3 September, a victim of American 55th Fighter Group P-51s. *Bundesarchiv*

Obstlt. Priller waits at the door of his headquarters trailer to meet arriving members of the Third Gruppe, looking much older than his twenty-eight years. Photographed at Lille-Nord, March or April 1944. *Bundesarchiv*

Maj. Mietusch takes off from Lille-Nord in his "Black 22" during March or April 1944. *Bundesarchiv*

A Third Gruppe "black man" (ground crewman) stands in front of his Bf 109G-6 in the spring of 1944. *Genth*

Chapter 8

The Invasion Front: June–December 1944

The Luftwaffe was totally surprised by the time and location of the Allied landing on the beaches of Normandy on 6 June 1944. Of JG 26's three Gruppen, one was resting in southern France and the other two had been dispersed inland. As a result, only two German fighters made an appearance over the Allied beachhead on D-Day morning—those of Obstlt. Priller and his wingman, Ogfr. Heinz Wodarczyk. By afternoon most of the home-based Jagdwaffe was *en route* to France to carry out the German defensive plan. Twenty Jagdgruppen were ultimately employed against the Allied invasion forces; all suffered terrible casualties. Many units

Ground crewmen help Obstlt. Priller from his FW 190A-8 *Jutta* during a visit to the Second Gruppe at Guyancourt, the first week after the Allied invasion of Normandy. *Bundesarchiv*

were reduced to a handful of aircraft in a few days and had to be ordered back to Germany. Except for one brief trip to Germany by the Second Gruppe for refitting, JG 26 remained on the Invasion Front for the entire campaign. Its pilots' skills in aerial ambushes and single-pass ground attacks, and its experienced ground staff's skills at camouflage and in-field maintenance, allowed JG 26 to retain a moderate level of effectiveness. Outnumbered in the air by twenty to one, German fighters were rarely visible to the ground forces of either the Allies or the Germans.

From airfields in the Paris region, JG 26 continued its vain struggle against the Allied armies until mid-August, when it was forced to join the general German retreat. The aircraft reached shelter behind the German border on 3 September. After the stabilization of the battle lines, JG 26 became the northernmost of the four Jagdgeschwader assigned to support the German Army along the Western Front, which stretched from the Netherlands to Switzerland. On 21 September the unit carried out the only successful Luftwaffe attack on the Allied air forces during Operation Market Garden (the airborne assault on the Rhine bridge at Arnhem) and downed twenty RAF transports.

Poor autumn weather and a shortage of aviation fuel restricted the Geschwader's missions during October and November. The first fields occupied by the Gruppen after their return to Germany all proved too wet, and the ground staffs located better bases for the winter. The First Gruppe moved to Fuerstenau; the

Second Gruppe personnel quickly push Obstlt. Priller's airplane under cover for the duration of his visit to their base at Guyancourt, June 1944. *Bundesarchiv*

Third Gruppe transferred to Plantluenne. The Second Gruppe was withdrawn to the interior to re-equip with the in-line-engined FW 190D-9, the latest version of the Focke-Wulf fighter, and on its return to the front was based at Nordhorn-Clausheide. The First Gruppe then converted to the FW 190D-9 while remaining on duty at Fuerstenau, while the Third Gruppe obtained examples of the last version of the Bf 109 to see service, the Bf 109K-4.

The German offensive in the Ardennes required a maximum effort from the Luftwaffe from 17 December through year's end. The Geschwader was reasonably successful in its new fighters, considering the low state of training of most of its pilots and the Luftwaffe's permanent state of numerical inferiority. The Third Gruppe of JG 54 returned to the combat zone after converting to FW 190D-9s and was attached to JG 26 as a fourth

Gruppe. This Gruppe suffered fourteen fatalities, including its Kommandeur, on a single 29 December mission, and its effectiveness was permanently blunted.

The photographs show the effect of loss of air superiority on the ground routine: the aircraft were placed under camouflage the moment they landed, and much of the pilots' time on the ground was spent in the woods and forests. Good photographs of the Geschwader's late-1944 aircraft are scarce. The series of official photographs kept in the Bundesarchiv ends abruptly in early August 1944. Few photographs of aircraft were taken by men of the combat units. Photographic film was scarce, especially on the open market, and those pilots and ground crewmen able to get it were more interested in capturing the images of their friends and pets than inanimate objects such as aircraft.

The 5th Staffel's FW 190A-8 "White 4," W.Nr. 170609, is pushed into its dispersal at Guyancourt shortly after D-Day.

Fhr. Ulrich Frantz was killed in this aircraft on 14 June. *Bundesarchiv*

Obstlt. Priller is presented the traditional flowers after his 100th victory. The pilot he is facing is Hptm. Matoni, who led the Second Gruppe on the mission; seen in profile at the right is Ogfr. Wodarczyk, Priller's wingman. Photographed at Guyancourt, 15 June. *Bundesarchiv*

Priller's 100th victim. The wreckage of Lt. David McMurray's 492nd Bomb Group B-24J burns in the Allied beachhead. McMurray's crew bailed out safely, but were killed in the crash of another aircraft the following month. *Cranston*

Obstlt. Priller speaks informally to the formation leaders of the Third Gruppe at Villacoublay-Nord in June or July 1944. From left: Maj. Mietusch (KIA 17 Sep 44), Hptm. Paul Schauder, Priller, Oblt. Peter Reischer (KIA 18 Dec 44), unknown, Oblt. Gottfried "Cognac" Schmidt, Lt. Hermann Guhl, Lt. Dieter Voelmle, Oblt. Harald Lenz (KIA 1 Jan 45), and Oblt. Theobald Kraus. *Genth*

Lt. Glunz chats with a ground crewman beside his "Black 9"; its rudder displays sixty-two victories. Photographed at Guyancourt, second week of June. *Bundesarchiv*

The 11th Staffel's Uffz. Erhard Tippe, a favorite wingman of Maj. Mietusch. Tippe was taken prisoner after being shot down by No. 443 Sqd. (RCAF) Spitfires over the Normandy beachhead on 16 June. *Genth*

Maj. Staiger amuses himself watching a Gefreiter refuel a wood-burning automobile. *Genth*

135

Lt. Georg Kiefner, 1st Staffel Kapitaen, and his FW 190A-8
"White 5," W.Nr. 171079, photographed on 24 June, the day
of its receipt by Kiefner. *Kiefner*

Another photograph of Kiefner's new FW 190A-8 at Boissy-
le-Bois, 24 June. *Kiefner*

The 4th Staffel's Uffz. Hermann Grad is greeted by his crew chief after returning from his first victorious combat. Photographed at Boissy-le-Bois, 25 June. *Schmidt via Meyer*

"Blue 10" and "Blue 18," 12th Staffel Bf 109G-6s or G-14s, photographed during an Alarmstart (scramble) in mid-1944. *Genth*

Uffz. Grad is congratulated on his first victory, the destruction of Lt. J. D. Coffman's crippled 489th Bomber Group B-24. Grad was himself killed over the Ardennes on 26 December by American 361st Fighter Group P-51s. *Schmidt*

Lt. Gerhard Vogt's FW 190A-8 "Brown 13," W.Nr. 170661, has its engine changed at Guyancourt. The photo was taken between 20 June, when Vogt took command of the 7th Staffel, and 5 July, when Vogt struck power lines during a forced landing after a battle with Spitfires, and destroyed the aircraft. *Meyer*

Another view of Lt. Vogt's FW 190A-8. *Sy*

Maj. Borris's FW 190A-7 has a tire changed; the spiral spinner dates the event as probably later than 25 June 1944, when this identification marking was ordered by Luftflotte 3. *Meyer*

Grad's Staffelkapitaen, Lt. Heinz Kemethmueller, pauses during the victory celebration at Boissy-le-Bois. Kemethmueller was an Eastern Front Knight's Cross winner who joined 7/JG 26 as an experienced reinforcement just before the Staffel transferred to Russia. He led the 4th Staffel from April 1944 until he was seriously injured in a ground accident in November. *Schmidt via Meyer*

"Black 18," a Bf 109G-6 of the 10th Staffel. Oblt. Fritz Bracher was killed in this aircraft on 17 July 1944. *Genth*

A Third Gruppe Bf 109G-6 in its dispersal. *Genth*

The 11th Staffel's Uffz. Ritter, Uffz. Heinz Gehrke's erste Wart (crew chief), with Gehrke's Bf 109G-6 "Yellow 1", nicknamed *Pikus*, which survived five or six weeks at the front before its destruction on the ground in a B-17 raid on Villacoublay airfield. The aircraft illustrates the markings changes ordered in late June for fighters in France—removal of the yellow paint on the undercowl and rudder, which had been the Channel Front theater markings since 1941, and repainting of the black-green spinner in black, with a white spiral. *Gehrke*

A movement of the 12th Staffel by French rail, some time in 1944. Oblt. Schrader is in the passenger seat of the tracked motorcycle, or "Krad." *Genth*

This desolate field of rubble is a fully functioning JG 26 air base in the Paris region, photographed during a tour by Genmaj. Galland in mid-July. *Bundesarchiv*

A 1st Staffel Rotte takes off for a ground-attack mission, carrying drop tanks and WGr. 21 rockets. Photographed at Les Mesnuls, August 1944. *Meyer*

Obstlt. Priller; Genmaj. Adolf Galland, General of the Fighter Arm; and Obst. Hannes Trautloft, Inspector of Day Fighters, on a visit to the Invasion Front in mid-July. *Bundesarchiv*

Oblt. Fred Heckmann and Lt. Karl-Heinz Kempf study their mission maps at Le Perray; quadrant "CR" is due north of Rennes. Heckmann was an Eastern Front Knight's Cross winner who joined the First Gruppe before its own Russian tour. He led the 3rd Staffel from January 1944 until March 1945, when he took over the 5th Staffel. *Bundesarchiv*

The 1st Staffel on the Invasion Front. From left: unknown, unknown, Uffz. Schwan, Obfw. Heinrich Teilken (KIA 21 Oct 44), Lt. Kiefner; far right, Lt. Friedrich Ramthun. *Meyer*

Oblt. Heckmann with two young First Gruppe Unteroffiziere, both wearing new Iron Crosses Second Class; these were invariably awarded immediately after a pilot's first victory, so these men can be identified from the victory records as Uffz. Werner Schwan (KIA 23 Sep 44) and Uffz. Otto Horch (KIA 19 Aug 44), and the photo can be dated as 8 August 1944, when the Gruppe was based at Le Perray. The two pilots downed P-51s from the American 359th Fighter Group. *Bundesarchiv*

Maj. George-Peter Eder, who succeeded Hptm. Emil Lang as Second Gruppe Kommandeur after the latter was killed during the 3 September transfer flight to Germany. Eder joined the Second Gruppe on 11 August as a post-D-Day reinforcement, and left in October to join Kommando Nowotny, the first jet fighter unit. *Eder*

The 7th Staffel's FW 190A-8 "Brown 6," W.Nr. 175140. This "pilot's monument" was abandoned by the unit on Mels-broek airfield near Brussels on 3 September, during the unit's retreat to Germany. *Air Force Museum*

Fw. Ungar shows off his FW 190D-9 to Struppi. Ungar's Gruppe, III/JG 54, long associated with JG 26, was the first service unit to begin converting to the FW 190D. Photographed at Hesepe, September. *Ungar*

A 9/JG 54 mechanic shows Struppi the supercharger air intake on an FW 190D-9 at Hesepe in September. *Ungar*

143

An October mission briefing for the 7th and 8th Staffeln at Stevede-Coesfeld, faked for the newsreels after presentation of the Knight's Cross to Oblt. Wilhelm Hofmann. From left: Lt. Gottfried Dietze, Uffz. Erich Ahrens (POW 1 Jan 45), Uffz. Heinz Meihs (KIA 13 Mar 45), Oblt. Hofmann (KIA 26 Mar 45), Lt. Bruno Mischkot (KIA Apr 45), Ogfr. Otto Puschenjack (KIA 22 Mar 45), Lt. Peter Andel, Ofhr. Gerhard Schulwitz (KIFA 25 Mar 45), Lt. Siegfried Sy, Uffz. Walter Stumpf, Uffz. Artur Fritsch (KIA 21 Oct 44). *Stumpf*

Fw. Fritz Ungar, a pilot in III/JG 54, sits in his FW 190D-9 with Staffelhund Struppi during the Gruppe's conversion training at Hesepe in September. *Ungar*

The Second Gruppe flew this FW 190D-9 while in conversion training at Reinsehlen in November. *Sy*

Hptm. Walter Krupinski, photographed at Plantluenne in late 1944. Krupinski won the Knight's Cross with Oak Leaves while serving with JG 52 on the Eastern Front. He transferred into JG 26 as Third Gruppe Kommandeur after Maj. Mietusch's death in September. Krupinski joined Genlt. Galland's jet unit, JV 44, after the Third Gruppe's dissolution in March 1945. *Genth*

The 7th Staffel's Uffz. Ahrens in a light moment at Stevede-Coesfeld, looking much like Slim Pickens in the movie *Dr. Strangelove. Stumpf*

Uffz. Meihs, Lt. Andel, Lt. Dietze, Uffz. Stumpf, and Uffz. Leopold Speer (KIA 1 Jan 45) pose in front of the 8th Staffel dispersal area at Stevede-Coesfeld in October. *Sundermann*

The 4th Staffel's Uffz. Hans Kukla. Kukla received the abbreviated training course typical of the Nachwuchs ("new growth") replacements, but was atypical in that he survived the war, albeit with injuries. *Kukla*

The 4th Staffel in a posed briefing scene, photographed at Fuerstenau on 10 December. From left: Lt. Waldemar Soeffing (Kapitaen), Uffz. Ludwig Sattler (KIA 26 Dec 1944), unknown, Gefr. Reinhard Anselment (KIA 10 Dec 1944), Uffz. Franz Weiss, Uffz. Hans Kukla, unknown, Uffz. Hermann Grad (KIA 26 Dec 1944). *Kukla*

Obfw. Karl Laub, one of the Third Gruppe's "old hares," so-called for their cautious tactics and erratic courses in the combat zone. He was killed in combat with No. 56 Sqd. (RAF) Tempests on 14 December 1944. *Genth*

A November consultation at the III/JG 54 base at Varrelbusch, where the Gruppe was completing its conversion training on the FW 190D-9. From left: a Junkers engineer, Lt. Crump, Lt. Theo Nibel (POW 1 Jan 45). The newly-commissioned Peter Crump joined III/JG 54 in mid-July 1944 in exchange for Hptm. Emil Lang, who replaced Hptm. Naumann as Kommandeur of II/JG 26. *Crump*

An early production FW 190D-9 flown by the Second Gruppe at Reinsehlen. *Sy*

Chapter 9

The Final Battles: 1945

The last major operation of the Jagdwaffe took place on New Year's Day 1945. This was Operation Bodenplatte (Baseplate), a mass attack on sixteen Allied tactical airfields in the Netherlands, Belgium, and eastern France. The mission cost the Luftwaffe 214 pilots, including thirty-two members of JG 26 and III/JG 54. The Allies replaced the 300 aircraft it lost on the ground within a week; the Jagdwaffe was weakened beyond any hope of recovery by the loss of so many of its pilots and experienced formation leaders.

When the Third Gruppe finished its conversion to FW 190D-9s in early February, the Geschwader was fully equipped with the Luftwaffe's best piston-engined fighter in service. The Schlageter fighters' mission for the rest of the war was ground support. They patrolled their own lines and attempted to ambush Allied artillery spotters and fighter bombers. During Allied ground offensives the pilots flew armed reconnaissance, attacked ground targets with rockets and bombs, and escorted other ground attack units. Pilots and aircraft were lost on nearly every mission and could no longer be replaced. Aircraft serviceability and fuel inventories also decreased, as the German transport system began to break down. In mid-February the 4th and 8th Staffeln were forced to disband. On 25 February III/JG 54 was redesignated as IV/JG 26, formalizing the relationship that had existed since the previous December.

On 25 March the Geschwader was forced by the advancing Allies to abandon its winter bases. The First, Second, and Fourth Gruppen pulled back deeper into Germany, but the Third Gruppe was disbanded; its personnel joined the surviving Gruppen. The Fourth Gruppe was disbanded on 17 April, leaving the Geschwader with two Gruppen, each containing three Staffeln. JG 26 continued its retreat ahead of the British Army, flying daily armed reconnaissance missions in ever-decreasing strength until the armistice on 4 May, which found the Geschwader on fields in Schleswig, near the Danish border. The Geschwader had claimed 2,700 aerial victories in five years of continuous combat; 763 Schlageter pilots had lost their lives.

The photographs continue the trend begun the preceding year; few photos were taken by the men of the Geschwader, and these very rarely featured the unit's aircraft. Photo documentation of JG 26's FW 190Ds comes primarily from two sources: Allied servicemen's photographs of Luftwaffe wrecks, and the Allied air forces, which preserved several FW 190Ds for testing. Of the four FW 190Ds brought to the United States after the war, three were from JG 26, including that rarest of the rare, the FW 190D-13 assigned to Maj. Franz Goetz, the Geschwader's last Kommodore; only a handful of FW 190D-13s reached the front, and Goetz's airplane is the only one to have survived or known to have been documented in photographs.

The remains of Lt. Elmer Clarey's 2nd Air Division B-24 after JG 26's attack on Brussels-Evere airfield during Operation Bodenplatte on New Year's Day. *Clarey*

Lt. Theo Nibel's FW 190D-9 after partial dismantling by the British. Nibel, a Schwarmfuehrer (flight leader) in Lt. Peter Crump's 10/JG 54, was captured during Operation Boden-platte after his engine cut out near Grimberghen airfield—a partridge had lodged in his radiator. *Air Force Museum*

Josef Priller is seen here after his promotion to Oberst on 1 January. *Gehrke*

7th Staffel FW 190D-9s taxi to takeoff position on a wood-paved strip at Nordhorn-Clausheide in January. *Poelchau*

Another view of the 7th Staffel's FW 190D-9s at Nordhorn-Clausheide. *Poelchau*

A dummy Ju 88, bait for a flak trap at Nordhorn-Clausheide airfield. *Poelchau*

Lt. Gerhard Vogt, a pilot in the Second Gruppe from his arrival as an Obergefreiter in the autumn of 1941 until his death while Kapitaen of the 5th Staffel. Vogt was credited with forty-eight victories in 174 combat flights, and was awarded the Knight's Cross. He was one of twelve JG 26 pilots killed on 14 January 1945. *Crump*

Three 14th Staffel pilots relax in the February sun at Varrelbusch. From left: Obfw. Werner Zech, Fw. Otto Weber, Obfw. Fritz Ungar. *Ungar*

Maj. Franz Goetz, Maj. Anton Hackl, and Obst. Priller (from left to right) during the modest ceremony marking Goetz's assumption of the command of JG 26 at Fuerstenau on 28 January. Goetz began the war as a Feldwebel in JG 53 and had spent the entire war with that Geschwader. Hackl had succeeded Eder in command of the Second Gruppe in October 1944, and was himself ordered away from JG 26 on the day after this ceremony to take command of JG 300. *Stumpf*

The north flak tower at the Third Gruppe's Plantluenne base was manned by these schoolboys. This 2cm gun has six victory rings on the gun's barrel. The gunlayer is Georg Ahlers, who received the Iron Cross for exceptional bravery as a Flakhelfer. The wooden block on the right side of the parapet is a zone of fire limiter, to prevent the gun from firing into the barracks. *Eickhoff*

The 5th Staffel's Lt. Gerhard "Bubi" Schulwitz, a popular and gifted pilot who was killed in a collision with his wingman after taking off on 25 March to transfer from Nordhorn-Clausheide to Bissel. *Crump*

Lt. Waldemar Radener, a long-serving Second Gruppe pilot who led the 7th Staffel in 1944 and succeeded Maj. Hackl as Kommandeur; he followed Hackl to JG 300 on 22 February 1945, and soon thereafter received his Knight's Cross. *Meyer*

Oblt. Wilhelm Hofmann, 8th Staffel Kapitaen until its disbandment and Vogt's successor at 5th Staffel. Hofmann joined the Second Gruppe in 1942 as an Unteroffizier and was killed on 26 March 1945, shot down accidentally by his own wingman. He was credited with forty-four victories in 260 combat flights and flew combat missions even after he was blinded in one eye in a ground accident in October 1944. *Crump*

Two members of the RCAF pose beside a wrecked FW 190D-9 formerly belonging to 7/JG 26; the brown Gruppe bar can be seen in front of the black/white rear fuselage Reichsverteidigung bands. *Hildebrandt*

Two Fourth Gruppe FW 190D-9s destroyed by their owners before abandoning Friesoythe. The nearest is W.Nr. 210148. *Public Archives of Canada*

Canadian troops examine the fuselage of a Fourth Gruppe FW 190D-9 in a hangar near Wilhelmshaven. The curved

Fourth Gruppe bar on the fuselage band appears to be yellow, the color of the 15th Staffel. *Public Archives of Canada*

The 10th Staffel's FW 190D-9 "Black 10," W.Nr. 500613, found by the Allies after being abandoned at Celle, northeast of Hannover. *Hildebrandt*

Remnants of the Second Gruppe after flying into internment at Kristiansand, Norway, on 5 May 1945. From left: Uffz. Willibald Malm, unknown, Gefr. Trautvetter, Lt. Jan Schild, Fw. Hermann Sinz, Uffz. Johannes Hoffmann. *Genth*

The 10th Staffel's "Black 10" displays a US identification number in preparation for shipment to the United States. Its fate is unknown, and it may have been scrapped in Europe. *Hildebrandt*

Geschwaderstab FW 190D-9 "Black 5," W.Nr. 401392, photographed on 24 September 1945. Note that the Stab's horizontal bar markings were still in use at war's end. The aircraft was shipped to the United States for evaluation, but its ultimate fate is unknown. *N.A.S.M.*

Flt. Lt. J.W.C. "Pee-Wee" Judge of No. 245 Sqd. (RAF), photographed on "Brown 18," an FW 190D-9 formerly of the 7th Staffel—Schleswig, summer 1945. *Browne via Thomas*

The final resting place of Pips Priller's last FW 190A-8 *Jutta*—a junk pile in Flensburg in the summer of 1945. *Fraser via Thomas*

Chapter 10

Camouflage And Markings

The camouflage schemes and the unit and personal markings of the Luftwaffe's fighter aircraft are a continued subject of study and dispute five decades after the war. The markings of the German fighter force were as colorful and diverse as those of any of the combatants. Their ability to fascinate the enthusiast and historian are attributable in part to the scarcity of official documentation, and in part to the apparent willingness of the front-line units to interpret the official guidelines very broadly. Credible first-hand data is scarce; veterans' memories of fifty-year-old paint schemes would be suspect even if the information had been considered especially significant at the time, which it was not. The researcher's principal sources of information about color schemes are a few documents, a few paint chips, a few relics, and the photographs that survived the war. The interpretation of colors from black-and-white photos will always be subject to personal bias. Thus, the controversies will never end.

This chapter will concentrate on topics specific to JG 26 and is not intended to be a comprehensive guide to Luftwaffe markings. Readers desiring more general or complete information should consult the excellent references listed in the bibliography. Jagdgeschwader 26 flew every model of every Luftwaffe single-piston-engined fighter to see front-line service, and a detailed study of this one unit has a better chance of reaching conclusions of general validity than a shallower study of broader scope. The subjects of the color paintings have been especially selected to show the greatest possible range of aircraft types and markings variations within the Geschwader, but these aircraft were in general less colorful than the fighters of many other Jagdgeschwader. Since the men of JG 26 considered themselves to be among the elite of the Luftwaffe, they saw no need to draw attention to themselves with gaudy paint schemes. For the last four years of the war they didn't even paint unit emblems on their aircraft—after all, *they* knew who they were. From 1941 to 1945 the finishes of JG 26's

aircraft were among the least individualistic and flamboyant in the Jagdwaffe, which ironically makes a study of this unit especially valuable—it provides a stable benchmark against which to check the dates of implementation and the details of interpretation of the official painting and markings guidelines.

Prewar through 1939

The Luftwaffe's first fighters were painted in an overall pale gray finish. They displayed civilian registration codes on the wings and fuselage; the new national emblem, the swastika, in a red band on the left side of the vertical tail; and the national colors, black, white, and red, in horizontal bands on the right side of the tail. On 1 June 1936, shortly after III/JG 134 had settled in at Cologne, the civilian codes were replaced with a complex military registration system comprising four digits and one letter; the swastika displaced the riband of national colors from the tail; and the Balkenkreuz, or straight-armed cross, made its appearance on wings and fuselage. On 1 September 1936, the system of identity codes changed yet again. The Gruppe, Staffel, and identity of each airplane in a Jagdgeschwader could now be distinguished by the color, shape, and location of geometric symbols and numerals painted on its fuselage. The Geschwader was identified by a distinctive color on its aircraft cowlings; the color assigned to JG 234, JG 26's direct predecessor, was orange. This system lasted only a year. Details will not be given here; interested readers are referred to the book by Fleuret.

Figure 1 depicts the He 51B of I/JG 234's first Kommandeur, Hptm. Oskar Dinort, in the full markings of the period. The orange cowling denotes the Geschwader. The white chevron and horizontal bars are the markings specified for the Geschwaderkommodore, which JG 234 had not yet been assigned. Although some references state that the official color for fighters at this time was RLM gray 02, a medium gray with a definite green cast, the photographic evidence indicates that most fighters, including this one, were still finished in neutral light gray.

The next major change in fighter markings came in 1937, with the introduction of the Bf 109B into service. All top and side surfaces of the new aircraft were painted in segments of black-green 70 and dark green 71. Undersurfaces were solid light blue 65. Identity codes were simplified yet again. The new system was documented in December 1937 in RLM Directive *Fl.In.3 Nr. 730/37 II*, which was followed closely by JG 26. This directive permitted the display of a Geschwader emblem in a specific 250mm-by-300mm area of the fuselage, in front of the cockpit. The Gruppe was denoted by a symbol behind the fuselage Balkenkreuz: no symbol for the First Gruppe, a horizontal bar for the Second Gruppe, and a vertical bar for the Third Gruppe. Aircraft identity numbers were located in front of the Balkenkreuz, and the aircraft number and Gruppe bar were painted in the Staffel color. The 1st, 4th, and 7th Staffeln had white codes with no outlines; the 2nd, 5th, and 8th Staffeln, red codes with white outlines; the 3rd, 6th, and 9th Staffeln, yellow codes with black outlines. *Figure 2* shows a Bf 109B of the 6th Staffel in early 1938. Note that the spinner is painted in the Staffel color, yellow.

The Geschwader and each Gruppe was led in the air by a staff flight of three aircraft (a Stabskette), which displayed distinctive geometric symbols. The aircraft of the Geschwader kommodore was to be marked with a single "Winkel" (chevron) followed by a pointed horizontal bar, the Balkenkreuz, and a second horizontal bar. The complete marking was called a "Pfeil" (arrow). The other two aircraft of this Kette were to be marked with the two bars and the Balkenkreuz only. The aircraft of each Gruppenkommandeur was to be marked with a chevron enclosing a small filled triangle—a "Winkel-Drieck." The other aircraft of the Gruppe Stabsketten bore a single chevron. Gruppe markings were carried behind the Balkenkreuz of the Gruppenstab aircraft, and all Stab identity markings were to be black, outlined in white. It is worth noting that the aircraft of the JG 26 Geschwaderstab carried the exact markings specified by the 1937 directive, with some additions, from 1938 to V-E Day. Gruppenstab aircraft also followed the directive closely. When the size of the Stab flights was increased from three to four aircraft in 1938, additional markings had to be found, but JG 26 kept these simple. The triple chevrons, circles, and other complex geometric figures used by some units were never applied to JG 26 aircraft—good evidence that they were never specified in an official directive.

At the time of the Sudeten crisis in August 1938, the horizontal red band and white circle surrounding the swastika on the Luftwaffe's aircraft were overpainted in camouflage greens, and the black swastika was given a thin white outline. Temporary tactical markings were employed during the many field maneuvers of 1938 and 1939; these consisted of various geometric markings as well as light-colored fuselage bands, tail units, and wing tips.

Figure 3 shows a Bf 109E-1 of the 2nd Staffel in early 1939. The Geschwader emblem has not yet been applied, but the aircraft displays an early example of a Staffel emblem. The latter were not specifically mentioned in the 1937 directive, but began appearing in large numbers in early 1939, apparently at the urging of pilots returning home after service in the Condor Legion in Spain. Combat in Spain was primarily by small formations, and it was felt important to foster unit pride at the Staffel level; the four German Jagdstaffeln in Spain all displayed unit badges.

The Schlageter Geschwader's badge, *Figure A*, was painted in front of the cockpits of all JG 26 aircraft in mid-1939, exactly in the location specified in the 1937 directive. It should be noted that wide variations existed in the shield's size and design; apparently no effort was made to standardize the stencils above the Staffel level. By the end of 1939 the aircraft of all but one of JG 26's ten Staffeln are known to have been displaying unit emblems. The aircraft of several pilots of the Geschwaderstab and Gruppenstaebe carried personal markings. No Gruppe emblems were developed or displayed, probably because the Geschwader was one of the first to be organized, and its Gruppen never led independent existences. All Staffel and personal emblems were initially painted beneath the cockpit; deviations from this location did not appear until mid-1940.

The Staffel emblems ran the usual gamut from the ferocious to the frivolous. The origins of several remain determinedly obscure. In the First Gruppe, Oblt. Franz Hoernig chose a grasshopper for his 1st Staffel *(Figure B)*; his successor, Oblt. Eberhard Henrici, replaced it with a more warlike spread-winged eagle. Hptm. Walter Kienitz's Red Devil *(Figure C)* was retained by his replacement at 2nd Staffel, Oblt. Fritz Losigkeit. The emblem's presentation increased in sophistication *(Figure D)* and moved to the nose of the aircraft during the course of 1940. Although at least two aircraft of Oblt. Johannes Seifert's 3rd Staffel displayed a bomb-carrying eagle *(Figure E)*, the survivors that have been queried state that this was not a Staffel emblem.

The aircraft of the Second Gruppe's Staffeln all displayed their emblems from late 1939 until they replaced their Bf 109Es with FW 190s in the autumn of 1941. The 4th Staffel lost its first emblem in September 1939 when most of its personnel left to form the 8th Staffel in the new Third Gruppe. The 4th Staffel's new Kapitaen, Hptm. Karl Ebbighausen, then chose a blocky caricature of a tiger's head to represent the unit *(Figure F)*. The 5th Staffel's emblem was one of the first chosen in the Geschwader. On his return from Spain in 1937 Oblt. Herwig Knueppel selected a cartoon character popular in the Condor Legion, the raven Hans Huckebein, for the 5th *(Figure G)*. The 6th Staffel's emblem was perhaps the most inspired choice of all. To the untrained eye it looks like a crudely drawn goat with absurdly large horns *(Figure H)*. However, Oblt. Alfred Pomaska's creation was a carefully designed cross between a chamois (fast and cunning) and an ibex (strong and combative)—a suitable symbol for a fighter pilot. It stood triumphantly on a globe, straddling Europe.

The three Staffeln of the Third Gruppe adopted symbols soon after they were formed in September 1939 and made widespread use of them on their aircraft and equipment. Oblt. Georg Beyer's 7th Staffel became the "Red Heart" Staffel *(Figure I)*. Its emblem moved in mid-1940 from beneath the cockpit to the nose, within a scalloped white surround. The emblem disappeared when the cowlings were painted yellow in the autumn of 1940, but emerged the following spring, without the white surround. The 8th Staffel received its Kapitaen, pilots, ground staff, and even its nickname by transfer from the 4th Staffel. Oblt. Edu Neumann, inspired by the popularity of Mickey Mouse among the Condor Legion veterans, adopted another cartoon character as an appropriate symbol for his 4th Staffel and took it with him to the 8th *(Figure J)*. He made it known that his choice, Adamson, was a good German rather than an American. Oblt. Gerhard Schoepfel's 9th Staffel adopted a red griffin, in German a "Hollenhund" or hellhound. The emblem's evolution from late 1939 to mid-1940 is apparent in the paintings *(Figures K, L)*.

The emblem of the night fighting Staffel, 10(Nacht)/ JG 26, was an arching black cat, which appeared on many Staffel aircraft. This Staffel's aircraft bore identity codes consisting of a white letter "N" and an aircraft number.

The personal markings of a number of Geschwader pilots have been described in the enthusiast literature over the past thirty years, but few can be authenticated. Among the best known are the bull and mouse of Hptm. Ebbighausen (see, *e.g.*, *JG 26: Top Guns of the Luftwaffe*), and the "Schlageter knight" of Maj. Hans-Hugo Witt *(Figure M)*, long thought to be a personal marking, but now believed to denote the Geschwaderstab. The aircraft of Maj. Handrick and Oblt. Knueppel displayed top hats, symbolic of their pilots' service in Spain.

The Western Campaign

The photographs in Chapter 2 show how dramatically the appearance of the Geschwader's Bf 109Es was altered during the winter of 1939–40 by extending the undersurface color, light blue 65, up the sides of the aircraft. Close examination of the photographs shows that the upper surfaces were lightened at the same time—the black-green 70/dark green 71 segments were overpainted with dark green 71/green-gray 02. *Figure 4* shows the Bf 109E-1 of the Kommodore, Maj. Witt, during early 1940. It is finished in standard 71/02/65 camouflage and displays the "Pfeil," the Kommodore's identity marking; the Schlageter shield; and the Stab emblem, the Schlageter knight. Prior to the invasion of France and the Low Countries the swastikas on the aircraft's tails were relocated from the rudder hinge line to the fin. During the campaign victory, markings in the form of vertical bars began to appear on the aircraft, at first on the fins, and when these proved too confining, on the rudders. These bars were usually painted in black, but JG 26 also used red. Embellishments such as roundels, dates, and aircraft types were added to the bars by some of the ground crewmen; these can be seen in the photographs.

The Battle of Britain

The Geschwader's aircraft entered the Battle of Britain in standard 71/02/65 finish, but exceptions began appearing as early as August. Several clear photographs show that while Hptm. Adolf Galland was Third Gruppe Kommandeur, his Bf 109E was finished with a light gray mottle on the top surfaces of wings and fuselage, rather than the official segmented pattern. The aircraft lost by JG 26 pilots Fw. Karl Straub and Oblt. Hans Krug in late August and early September were described by RAF Intelligence as having a "gray speckled finish" on their top surfaces. Although mottled upper surfaces were never adopted by the RLM for day fighters, gray finishes were, and that autumn several RAF crash reports described Messerschmitts with two-tone segmented gray wings. These were the first examples of the Luftwaffe's next standard fighter camouflage finish—dark gray 74/gray 75 over light blue 76 undersurfaces. (Note that color 74 is sometimes referred to as "gray-green" and color 75 as "gray-violet"; also, light blue 76 is nearly identical to light blue 65.) Unfortunately, 74/75/76 is impossible to distinguish from 71/02/65 in black-and-white photographs, but from the written evidence this was an uncommon finish on JG 26 Bf 109Es until the very end of 1940.

The light blue sides of the Luftwaffe's Bf 109s provided an effective camouflage for fighter combat at high altitude, but were apparently too conspicuous when the fighters were forced into the role of close escort for the bombers. Fuselage camouflage went through three distinct phases during the Battle. Some units began darkening the sides of their Messerschmitts with hand-applied blotches, streaks, or washes of green-gray 02 as early as July. JG 26's First and Second Gruppen were darkening their aircraft by September, but much of the Third Gruppe resisted the trend until the end of the year. Some of the Third Gruppe's fuselages were dulled with thin washes of green-gray 02, but the aircraft of the 9th Staffel's Oblt. Heinz Ebeling and Fw. Walter Braun, which collided over England on 5 November, had the same light blue fuselage sides with which they had entered the Battle in July. One piece of conclusive evidence for the second scheme exists in the form of a color photograph of Hptm. Gerhard Schoepfel's Bf 109E-7, which during the winter of 1940–41 had 71/02 upper surfaces and a very pale green-gray 02 wash over the light blue 65 fuselage sides. The third fuselage finish was first seen in late 1940, and consisted of a sprayed mottle of gray 75 over a light blue 65 or light blue 76 base. Some aircraft arrived from the factory in this finish, and some, such as Adolf Galland's, were repainted by the units. It is probable that 74/75 segmented upper surfaces also made their appearance in JG 26 at this time, although conclusive evidence is lacking.

As the scale of the fighter combats over England increased in July and August, a means of quick identification in the air was needed; tactical markings in temporary yellow or white paint became common. Oblt. Werner Bartels, the Third Gruppe technical officer, was shot down on JG 26's first mission to England on 24 July in an aircraft with a yellow rudder, but this was probably a unit or personal marking, rather than a theater marking; the latter were first used on a broad scale in mid-August and initially took the form of yellow-tipped wings, rudders, and elevators. The nose was quickly added to the area painted; according to RAF reports, Messerschmitts with full yellow cowlings were being encountered frequently by late August. On 1 September the yellow paint was removed from most of the fighters and replaced with white wing and tail tips—Gefr. Peter Holzapfel's 7th Staffel aircraft had these white markings when it was shot down south of London on 6 September. A few days later, all white paint was removed, and cowlings and rudders were painted in yellow. Yellow cowlings and rudders remained the standard theater marking for German fighters for the rest of the Battle of Britain. The area around the victory bars on the rudder was first left in its original blue finish, but when the rudders were ultimately repainted with permanent yellow 04 paint the bars were repainted over the yellow base.

Staffel colors were used for the aircraft identity codes and, in some cases, the aircraft spinners. The colors of several Staffeln had changed since 1939. Red markings were officially discouraged, probably because of the chance of confusion with the red in the RAF's

roundel, and most "red" Staffeln, including JG 26's 5th and 8th, changed to black markings. The 2nd Staffel, however, retained its red codes at least through 1940. The 6th Staffel substituted brown 26 for its prescribed yellow 27 codes, probably owing to a temporary shortage of yellow paint. The Staffel liked the new color so much that it retained it for the rest of the war. Spinners all arrived from the factory in black-green 70, but many different paint schemes were applied in the theater, often incorporating the unit identity color. All-red spinners were common in the 2nd Staffel. A popular early scheme saw one-quarter of the spinner overpainted in white; this remained common in the "white" Staffeln, the 1st, 4th, and 7th. When the cowlings were painted yellow in September, many Staffeln overpainted the spinners in yellow as well; this appears to have been especially common in the "yellow" Staffeln, the 3rd, 6th, and 9th. The spinner caps issued to cover the hole originally intended for an engine cannon provided another source of variation; yellow spinners were sometimes capped with other colors.

Stab identity codes remained black, outlined in white, but the aircraft spinners of some Stab aircraft were painted in distinctive colors. The spinners of the First Gruppe Stabsschwarm were finished in blue, with white rings, while some aircraft of the Geschwaderstab had spinner caps in a medium hue; this was probably green, an official Stab color, rather than red as has often been reported. A table of 1940 JG 26 unit colors is given here for reference:

Jagdgeschwader 26 Unit Identification Colors September 1940

Geschwaderstab: green

First Gruppe	Second Gruppe	Third Gruppe
Stab: blue	Stab: unknown	Stab: unknown
1st Staffel: white	4th Staffel: white	7th Staffel: white
2nd Staffel: red	5th Staffel: black	8th Staffel: black
3rd Staffel: yellow	6th Staffel: brown	9th Staffel: yellow

Figure 5 depicts the aircraft of Oblt. Gerhard Schoepfel, Kapitaen of the 9th Staffel, as it appeared on the evening of 18 August. The yellow theater markings had been applied no more than a day previously. Camouflage is unmodified 71/02/65. The identity codes and fuselage Balkenkreuz are smaller than regulation, which was characteristic of Third Gruppe aircraft throughout the Battle. Schoepfel's aircraft is numbered "one," as were those of most Staffelkapitaene during 1940. His command pennant, a triangular piece of sheet metal painted in the Staffel color, is mounted on the radio mast. The practice of displaying the pennant as an aid to quick identification in combat was observed irregularly

by the Staffelkapitaene and died out entirely during 1941.

Figure 6 shows the aircraft of another Third Gruppe Kapitaen, Oblt. Micky Sprick of the 8th Staffel, as it appeared in late September. Its fuselage sides have been given a light wash of green-gray 02. The rudder has been painted yellow on either side of an original blue band containing the red victory bars. The cowling is not yellow, as would have been typical for the period, but it may have been a recent replacement, not yet overpainted.

Figure 7 shows Obstlt. Adolf Galland's aircraft after it had been repainted in the new gray scheme in December. Upper surfaces are probably segmented dark gray 74/gray 75; undersurfaces are light blue 65; fuselage sides are light blue 65 oversprayed with gray 75 mottle. His Kommodore markings follow the 1937 directive. The yellow rudder has not been completely repainted; the black victory bars are still on their original blue surround. The cowling, spinner, and spinner cap are all yellow. *Figure N* depicts the most famous personal emblem in the Luftwaffe, Galland's Mickey Mouse.

The Mediterranean Theater

The aircraft of the 7th Staffel reached Sicily in February 1941 in factory-fresh North European finish: dark gray 74/gray 75 upper surfaces, light blue 76 under surfaces, and gray 75 mottle over light blue 76 on the fuselage sides. Rudders and cowlings were painted with permanent yellow 04; spinners were three-quarters black-green 70 and one-quarter white 21. Identity codes consisted of standard-sized white numerals and a vertical white Third Gruppe bar. All aircraft displayed the Geschwader badge and the Staffel's Red Heart emblem. Soon after entering combat the Gruppe bars were overpainted with the newly specified theater marking, a white fuselage band. This was the only major change in the markings of the aircraft during their six months in the theater.

Figure 8 depicts Oblt. Joachim Muencheberg's aircraft as it appeared at the end of March 1941. His first missions from Sicily were flown in "White 1", but "White 12" soon became his regular aircraft; here it displays his command pennant.

The Channel Coast

When the Geschwader returned to France in the spring of 1941, its Messerschmitts were finished in a variety of schemes. Some of its Bf 109E-7s were still in 71/02/65 camouflage; others were in 74/75/76. The few Bf 109F-0s had a very pale finish, either 74/75/76 or 75/77/76 (color 77 was a light gray), with a light overspray of gray 75 on the fuselage. The first Bf 109F-2s to reach the Third Gruppe had very dark fuselage sides, probably from a heavy spray of green-gray 02. By June Bf 109F-2s were arriving at the front in a new standard camouflage scheme documented in a Messerschmitt painting chart dated 15 August 1941. The scheme was basically 74/75/76, but fuselage sides were to be sprayed with roughly equal amounts of green-gray 02, black-green 70, and dark gray 74. Spinners were to be two-thirds black-green 70 and one-third white 21, with light blue 76 tips, although totally black-green spinners were also common. Cowlings and rudders on the fighters of the Channel units were usually painted yellow, but by the end of 1941 the yellow on the noses of the aircraft was being restricted to the bottom panel of the cowling, beneath the exhaust stacks. The aircraft the Geschwader brought to France bore Geschwader and Staffel emblems, but these were apparently not painted on replacement aircraft, and by year's end no JG 26 aircraft carried them. It is tempting to speculate that security considerations prompted an order forbidding the display of unit emblems by the only two Jagdgeschwader left in France after the invasion of the Soviet Union, in an attempt to disguise the Luftwaffe's weakness in the Western theater. But the Kommodore of JG 26 at that time remembers no such order. Other JG 26 veterans recall that the times were too hectic for such niceties as unit emblems, but this may be a rationalization. For whatever reason, unit emblems were never again displayed on JG 26 aircraft.

Figure 9 depicts a typical Third Gruppe aircraft in Brittany in early 1941. Note the dark fuselage side, yellow cowling and rudder, and Geschwader and Staffel emblems. *Figure 10* depicts the aircraft of the First Gruppe Kommandeur after its force-landing in England on 10 July 1941. It is a good example of the new Messerschmitt camouflage scheme; the only unusual aspect of its markings is the lack of any yellow paint on the nose. *Figure 11* shows one of Obst. Galland's Bf 109F-2/U "Specials" as it appeared on the day of Galland's departure from the unit, 5 December 1941. It is painted in the now-standard five-color camouflage scheme, with yellow undercowl and rudder. There is no Schlageter shield, and Galland's Mickey Mouse faces left rather than his customary right. *Figure 12* shows a typical Bf 109F-4/B of the 10th Staffel, the Jabostaffel. The Messerschmitts of this Staffel carried white identity numbers and unit marking; the marking, a falling bomb, was behind the Balkenkreuz. When the Staffel converted to FW 190s, the color of the numerals and bomb marking was changed to black.

According to all of the available evidence, every FW 190A assigned to JG 26 from 1941 to the end of 1944 was camouflaged in a factory-applied finish comprising dark gray 74/gray 75 upper surfaces and light blue 76 sides and undersurfaces; the sides were darkened with spray-painted dark gray 74. Black-green 70 spinners and yellow 04 undercowls and rudders were standard from 1941 to D-Day and were found on nearly all aircraft. Allied reports of Channel front FW 190s with all-yellow cowlings or red cowlings and rudders have no basis in fact. A few aircraft displayed personal emblems, and most (but not all) successful pilots continued to paint victory bars on the rudders of their aircraft; red remained a popular color for these victory bars in JG 26.

The basic system of aircraft identity codes remained in use for the rest of the war, with some modifications over time. The Geschwaderstab used codes that were unique to JG 26. While the Kommodore's aircraft normally displayed the "Pfeil" insignia as before, the aircraft of his Stab had their pointed bar-Balkenkreuz-horizontal bar prefaced with one or two initials that were derived from the names of the pilots assigned to the Stab, whether or not those pilots flew combat missions. Obstlt. Galland was photographed exiting Bf 109F-4 "P" in 1941; Obfw. Gruenlinger was killed in FW 190A-5 "B" on 4 September 1943—so the system was used for at least two years. Known initials were:

B: Fliegerstabsingenieur Ernst Battmer (technical officer)
He: Obfw. Bruno Hegenauer (wingman)
G: Hptm. Wilhelm Gaeth (staff officer)
P: Hptm. Gerhard Philipp (operations officer)
S: Oblt. Wilfried Sieling (adjutant)
VH: Lt. Viktor Hilgendorff (staff officer)

The pointed bar-Balkenkreuz-horizontal bar marking continued to be applied to Stab aircraft even after the use of initials was discontinued.

Maj. Priller's aircraft showed some variations from the standard Kommodore marking. His first aircraft after he became Kommodore had a "Winkel-Drieck" (chevron-triangle) in front of the pointed bar, instead of a single chevron. He then flew an aircraft with a 13 painted in black in front of the bar, changed to an airplane with a conventional "Pfeil" marking, and finally converted to another "Black 13." The "13" may have been chosen to comply with an often-hypothesized order (as yet unlocated by this author) that formation leaders were to fly aircraft marked with numerical codes rather than command chevrons, which it could be assumed helped Allied fighter pilots identify their most valuable aerial targets.

Gruppe identity codes showed few changes. In late 1942 the 11th (Hoehen) Staffel used a black wavy line behind the Balkenkreuz as its unit marking. The three new Staffeln that joined the Geschwader in early 1943 may have used the wavy line marking for a while also—it was coming into use as a Fourth Gruppe code—and there is photographic evidence for its use by the new 12th Staffel.

The aircraft of the Gruppenkommandeure all displayed either a "Winkel-Drieck" or a "Doppel-Winkel" (double chevron) until 1944. In early 1944 the Second Gruppe's Kommandeur, Hptm. Johannes Naumann, flew a "Black 30," and his successor, Hptm. Emil Lang, was killed in "Green 1". Maj. Klaus Mietusch of the Third Gruppe flew several aircraft with black numbers in the twenties. Maj. Karl Borris of the First Gruppe was flying a "Doppel-Winkel" aircraft after D-Day and may have used that marking continuously.

From 1943 the aircraft of the Stab flights of all three Gruppen were denoted by single-digit green numerals, with or without chevrons. There were two known exceptions, both pertaining to the Third Gruppe: in mid-1943 its Stab used blue numerals with chevrons, and for a period in 1944, all aircraft of its Stab carried black numbers in the twenties, without chevrons.

After 1943 Staffelkapitaene rarely flew in aircraft numbered "one." It is not known if this was the consequence of a formal policy or simply a matter of personal preference. For a period in 1943, while the Geschwader was expanding to twelve Staffeln, the Staffel colors showed some anomalies, as is apparent from the following table:

Jagdgeschwader 26 Unit Identification Colors July 1943

Geschwaderstab: black

First Gruppe	Second Gruppe	Third Gruppe
Stab: green	Stab: green	Stab: blue
1st Staffel: white	4th Staffel: white	7th Staffel: white
2nd Staffel: black	5th Staffel: black	9th Staffel: yellow
3rd Staffel: yellow	6th Staffel: brown	11th Staffel: red
8th Staffel: black	10th Staffel: white	12th Staffel: blue

The Staffel numbers and colors were regularized during the October 1943 reorganization; the identity colors used from early 1944 until the final decline in 1945 are listed in the table below. Green is speculated for the Geschwaderstab based on a photo of a Stab aircraft with a highly non-standard spinner finish comprising a white spiral on a light-colored base; the only logical light color for the spinner at that time was green, blue having been appropriated by the fourth Staffeln of the Gruppen.

Jagdgeschwader 26 Unit Identification Colors March 1944-March 1945

Geschwaderstab: green

First Gruppe	Second Gruppe	Third Gruppe
Stab: green	Stab: black or green	Stab: black or green
1st Staffel: white	5th Staffel: white	9th Staffel: white
2nd Staffel: black	6th Staffel: black	10th Staffel: black
3rd Staffel: yellow	7th Staffel: brown	11th Staffel: yellow
4th Staffel: blue	8th Staffel: blue	12th Staffel: blue

Figure 13 is representative of the first FW 190As to reach the Geschwader in 1941. *Figure 14* is Lt. Hilgendorff's Geschwaderstab aircraft; it appeared in a 1942 newsreel, but has not to date been identified in any still photographs. *Figure 15* depicts one of the several aircraft assigned to Hptm. Priller when he was Third Gruppe Kommandeur. Note the black paint masking the exhaust stains. JG 26 frequently painted this area of its FW 190As and Bf 109Gs, and sometimes even outlined the black with white, but elaborate designs such as the often-photographed "exhaust eagle" were found only in JG 2. *Figure O* is Priller's famous ace of hearts emblem as it appeared on this aircraft. It was painted in some form on every aircraft Priller was assigned during the war. *Figure 16* is representative of a 1943 FW 190A in factory finish; it is a fairly late example of a "number one" assigned to a Staffelkapitaen. *Figure 17* depicts the light-weight drop tank rack common in JG 26, and a rudder marking common elsewhere, but unique within JG 26. Many Luftwaffe Experten displayed their Knight's Crosses on their rudders, along with a number representing the victories for which the award was granted. Adolf Glunz is the only JG 26 pilot known to have followed this practice after the departure of Adolf Galland. *Figures 19* and *20* depict two Third Gruppe Bf 109G-6s as they appeared on the same day in early 1944. Both are in standard factory finish. The former is one of Maj. Mietusch's aircraft; the latter is a typical Staffel aircraft.

The Eastern Front

The only photographs showing JG 26 aircraft on the Eastern Front that are known to this author are in the hands of a private collector who has not released them for publication. The fuselages of the First Gruppe's FW 190A-5s were in a green/gray segmented camouflage characteristic of JG 54, with which they shared the northern section of the front.

The Invasion Front

On 25 June 1944, the Allied ULTRA organization intercepted a Luftflotte 3 order to its fighter units in France calling on them to remove all old theater markings from their aircraft; the new theater marking was to be a white spiral on an otherwise black spinner. JG 26 quickly repainted the spinners of its FW 190As and Bf 109Gs, but in all probability did not bother to overpaint the old Channel front markings of yellow undercowls and rudders. Replacement aircraft in the new scheme were arriving well before 20 July, the date of the RLM order confirming Luftflotte 3's earlier actions. The subject of *Figure 18* is well known; it appears in an often-reprinted photograph from the Imperial War Museum. However, it has never before been properly identified, and is a perfect example of a post D-Day JG 26 FW 190A. *Figure 21* illustrates a hitherto-unknown aircraft in the only totally authenticated finish of a post D-Day Third Gruppe Bf 109 known to this author; it is especially unusual as it is an example of a JG 26 wingman's aircraft with personal markings. *Figure P* shows the aircraft's emblem—Pikus the tomcat. Pikus was not a cartoon character, but was entirely a product of the imagination of the aircraft's pilot, Uffz. Heinz Gehrke.

Final Days in The Homeland

In late 1944, the RLM published its last directive detailing the camouflage finishes to be applied to day fighters. It introduced several new colors by number; unfortunately, no color names or samples were provided with the directive, and the aircraft manufacturers were apparently left to their own interpretation. Late-war paint colors are still a matter of some contention among historians and enthusiasts. JG 26's FW 190Ds were probably finished in gray-violet 75/dark green 82 upper surfaces, and light blue 76 fuselage sides and undersurfaces, the sides being mottled with dark green 82 and/or gray-violet 75. The finish of the Third Gruppe's Bf 109G-14s and Bf 109K-4s, which were exchanged for FW 190Ds in early 1945, is unfortunately not a fit subject for speculation, as no photographs of these aircraft have been located.

At some undetermined time in December 1944 or early January 1945, the aircraft of JG 26 were painted with Reichsverteidigung (Defense of the Reich) bands—one black and one white band, each 450mm wide, encircling the fuselage just forward of the tail. Veterans recall that the FW 190Ds of the Second Gruppe as well as the Bf 109s of the Third Gruppe carried these bands during Operation Bodenplatte on New Year's Day. However, the only JG 26 aircraft type with bands documented in known photographs is the FW 190D. The earliest photos date from mid-January, after Bodenplatte, but well before 20 February, when the RLM's order mandating the bands was finally issued.

When III/JG 54 was attached to JG 26 on 25 February 1945 as its Fourth Gruppe, it was assigned the standard late-war Fourth Gruppe symbol, a wavy horizontal line. This was quickly applied to its aircraft, along with aircraft identity numbers in the new colors, which were: 13th Staffel, white; 14th Staffel, black; 15th Staffel, yellow.

Maj. Franz Goetz, the Geschwader's last Kommodore, continued the unit's practice of adopting slightly unusual Stab markings for its leader's aircraft; his displayed yellow numerals in addition to the two standard black horizontal bars. Little information is available on the markings of the Gruppenstab aircraft. There is no authenticated example of a JG 26 FW 190D with chevron Stab markings; the Third Gruppe Stab is known to have used green identity numbers on its FW 190Ds. The last Staffelkapitaen known to have flown a "number one" was the 2nd Staffel's Oblt. Franz Kunz, who was injured in FW 190D-9 "Black 1" during Bodenplatte.

Figure 22 is an early production FW 190D-9 that was flown by the Second Gruppe during its conversion training; it is not believed to have seen combat with the unit. Its camouflage finish is factory standard; a unique feature of its markings is the location of its aircraft identity number on the rudder. *Figure 23* is a Third Gruppe aircraft that was abandoned on a junk pile and was photographed there by Allied servicemen; it is representative of the Geschwader's FW 190D-9s in service. *Figure 24* is Maj. Goetz's FW 190D-13, which survived the war and is presently on display at the Champlin Fighter Museum in Mesa, Arizona. The ace of spades is symbolic of Goetz's long service with JG 53, the "Pik-As" or "Ace of Spades" Geschwader. The aircraft's original colors and markings were recently authenticated by artist Jerry Crandall by sampling through the layers of paint applied since the war; the painting should thus be regarded as highly accurate.

Appendices

Sources

Research for this book required a thorough study of the voluminous literature on the Messerschmitt Bf 109, the Focke-Wulf FW 190, and Luftwaffe camouflage and markings. The books listed below were found especially valuable and are recommended.

Barbas, B. *Planes of the Luftwaffe Fighter Aces Vols. 1 & 2*. Kookaburra (Melbourne), 1985.

Beaman, J. & Campbell, J. *Messerschmitt Bf 109 in Action Part 1*. Squadron/Signal (Carrollton, TX), 1980.

Beaman, J. *Messerschmitt Bf 109 in Action Part 2*. Squadron/Signal (Carrollton, TX), 1983.

Caldwell, D. L. *JG 26: Top Guns of the Luftwaffe*. Orion Books (New York), 1991.

Campbell, J. *Focke Wulf FW 190 in Action*. Squadron/Signal (Carrollton, TX), 1975.

Fleuret, A. *Luftwaffe Camouflage 1935–1940*. Kookaburra (Melbourne), 1981.

Frappé, J-B. *La Luftwaffe attack a l'ouest (France 1939–1942)*. Éditions Heimdal (Bayeux, France), 1991.

Frappé, J-B. *La Luftwaffe en France 2. Normandie 1944*. Éditions Heimdal (Bayeux, France), 1989.

Green, W. *Augsburg Eagle*. Doubleday (New York), 1971.

Green, W. *Warplanes of the Third Reich*. Doubleday (New York), 1972.

Held, W. *Adolf Galland: Ein Fliegerleben in Krieg und Frieden*. Podzun-Pallas-Verlag (Friedberg), 1983.

Hildebrandt, C. *Broken Eagles 1: FW 190D*. Fighter Pictorials (Perkiomenville, PA), 1987.

Hitchcock, T. *Gustav—Messerschmitt 109G Parts 1 & 2*. Monogram (Boylston, MA), 1977.

Kit, M. & Aders, G. *Les Messerschmitt sur le front méditerranéen*. Éditions Atlas (Paris), 1982.

Lorant, J-Y. & Frappé, J-B. *Le Focke-Wulf 190*. Éditions Larivière (Paris), 1981.

Merrick, K. A. & Hitchcock, T. H. *The Official Monogram Painting Guide to German Aircraft 1935–1945*. Monogram (Boylston, MA), 1980.

Nauroth, H. *Die deutsche Luftwaffe vom Nordkap bis Tobruk 1939–1945*. Pozun-Pallas-Verlag (Friedberg), ca. 1980.

Nowarra, H. *Die 109*. Motorbuch (Stuttgart), 1979.

Nowarra, H. *Focke Wulf FW 190—Ta 152*. Motorbuch (Stuttgart), 1987.

Obermaier, E. *Die Ritterkreuztraeger der Luftwaffe: Jagdflieger 1939–1945*. Verlag Dieter Hoffman (Mainz), 1966.

Payne, M. *Bf 109—Into the Battle*. Air Research Publications (Surbiton, UK), 1987.

Payne, M. & Kit, M. *Les Messerschmitt dans la bataillle d'Angleterre*. Éditions Atlas (Paris), 1980.

Prien, J. & Rodeike, P. *Messerschmitt Bf 109F, G, & K Series: An Illustrated Study*. Schiffer (Atglen, PA), 1993.

Priller, J. *JG 26: Geschichte eines Jagdgeschwaders.*. Kurt Vowinckel Verlag (Heidelberg), 1956.

Ries, K. *Markings and Camouflage Systems of Luftwaffe Aircraft in World War II Vols. I–IV*. Verlag Dieter Hoffmann (Mainz), 1963–1969.

Ries, K. *Dora Kurfuerst und rote 13. Ein Bildband: Flugzeuge der Luftwaffe 1933–1945*. Verlag Dieter Hoffmann (Mainz), 1964.

Ries, K. *Luftwaffen Story 1935–1939*. Verlag Dieter Hoffmann (Mainz), 1974.

Ries, K. *Luftwaffe Embleme 1935–1945*. Verlag Dieter Hoffmann (Mainz), 1976.

Ries, K. *Luftwaffe Photo-Report 1939–1945*. Motorbuch Verlag (Stuttgart), 1984.

Smith, J. & Creek, E. *FW 190D*. Monogram (Boylston, MA), 1986.

Smith, J. & Gallaspy, J. *Luftwaffe Camouflage & Markings Vols. 2 & 3*. Kookaburra (Melbourne), 1976.

Vanackere, E. *von Flugplatz tot Airport: de geschiedenis van het vliegeld Bissegem-Wevelgem*. Privately published (Kortrijk, Belgium), 1991.

Table Of Equivalent Ranks— GAF, USAAF, and RAF

GAF Title	GAF Abbr.	USAAF Title	USAAF Abbr.	RAF Title	RAF Abbr.
Commisioned Officers					
Reichsmarschall					
Generalfeldmarschall		General (5 star)	Gen.	Marshal of the RAF	
Generaloberst	Genobst.	General (4 star)	Gen.	Air Chief Marshal	
General der Flieger	Gen. der Flg.	Lieutenant General	Lt. Gen.	Air Marshal	
Generalleutnant	Genlt.	Major General	Maj. Gen.	Air Vice Marshal	
Generalmajor	Genmaj.	Brigadier General	Brig. Gen.	Air Commodore	Air Cdre.
Oberst	Obst.	Colonel	Col.	Group Captain	Gp. Capt.
Oberstleutnant	Obstlt.	Lieutenant Colonel	Lt. Col.	Wing Commander	Wing Cdr.
Major	Maj.	Major	Maj.	Squadron Leader	Sqd. Ldr.
Hauptmann	Hptm.	Captain	Capt.	Flight Lieutenant	Flt. Lt.
Oberleutnant	Oblt.	First Lieutenant	1st Lt.	Flying Officer	Flg. Off.
Leutnant	Lt.	Second Lieutenant	2nd Lt.	Pilot Officer	Plt. Off.
Warrant Officers					
Stabsfeldwebel	Stabsfw.	Flight Officer	Flt. Off.	Warrant Officer	Wt. Off.
Oberfaehnrich	Ofhr. (Sr. Off. Candidate)				
Noncommissioned Officers					
Hauptfeldwebel	Hptfw.	Sergeant Major	Sgt. Maj.		
Oberfeldwebel	Obfw.	Master Sergeant	MSgt.	Flight Sergeant	Flt. Sgt.
Faehnrich (Fahnenjunker)	Fhr. (Officer Candidate)				
Feldwebel	Fw.	Technical Sergeant	TSgt.	Sergeant	Sgt.
Unterfeldwebel	Ufw.	Sergeant	Sgt.		
Unteroffizier	Uffz.	Corporal	Cpl.	Corporal	Cpl.
Enlisted Ranks					
Hauptgefreiter	Hptgefr.				
Obergefreiter	Ogfr.			Leading Aircraftsman	
Gefreiter	Gefr.	Private 1st Class	PFC.	Aircraftsman 1st Cl.	
Flieger	Flg.	Private	Pvt.	Aircraftsman 2nd Cl.	

Glossary

Balkenkreuz: "girder cross" or straight-armed cross—the German national insignia.

Blitzkrieg: "lightning war"—the highly mobile form of warfare practiced by the Wehrmacht between 1939 and 1941—featured close cooperation between armored and air forces.

Drieck: triangle.

erste Wart: crew chief.

Ergaenzungsgruppe (ErgGr): advanced training group.

Flugzeugfuehrer: pilot.

freie Jagd: "free hunt"—a fighter sweep without ground control.

Fuehrer: leader.

Fuehrungsstaffel: leader's squadron.

Geschwader: wing (pl. **Geschwader**)—the largest mobile, homogeneous Luftwaffe flying unit.

Geschwaderkommodore: wing commodore—usually a Major, Oberstleutnant, or Oberst in rank.

Geschwaderstab: the Geschwader staff.

Gruppe (Gr): group (pl. **Gruppen**)—the basic Luftwaffe combat and administrative unit.

Gruppenkommandeur: group commander—usually a Hauptmann, Major, or Oberstleutnant in rank.

Gruppenstab: the Gruppe staff.

Jabostaffel: fighter-bomber squadron.

Jaeger: originally, a hunter; now, also, a fighter pilot.

Jagdbomber (Jabo): fighter-bomber.

Jagdflieger: fighter pilot(s).

Jagdfliegerfuehrer (Jafue): fighter command/control unit or its commander. The Jafue originated as administrative units, but evolved into operational control units during the war.

Jagdgeschwader (JG): fighter wing, commanding three or four Gruppen. The authorized strength of JG 26 ranged from 124 to 208 fighters during the war.

Jagdgruppe (JGr): fighter group, containing three or four Staffeln. The authorized strength of a JG 26 Gruppe ranged from forty to sixty-eight fighters during the war.

Jagdschutz: "fighter protection"—generally, a patrol of a section of front, rather than an escort mission.

Jagdstaffel: fighter squadron, originally containing twelve aircraft (three Schwaerme). Its authorized strength was increased to sixteen aircraft in 1943.

Jagdwaffe: fighter arm or fighter force.

Kanalfront: the (English) Channel front.

Kanalgeschwader: the Geschwader serving on the English Channel (JG 2 and JG 26).

Kanaljaeger: fighter pilot(s) based near the Channel.

Kapitaen: captain. A position rather than a rank; a Staffel was commanded by a Kapitaen.

Kette: flight of three aircraft.

Kommandeur: commander. A position rather than a rank; a Gruppe was commanded by a Kommandeur.

Kommodore: commodore. A position rather than a rank; a Geschwader was commanded by a Kommodore.

Luftflotte (LF): air fleet; corresponded to a numbered American air force.

Luftwaffe: air force—the German Air Force is implied.

Nachwuchs: "new growth"—a late-war replacement pilot.

Oberkommando der Luftwaffe (OKL): the Luftwaffe High Command.

Oberwerkmeister: line chief.

Pfeil: arrow.

Reich: empire—Hitler's Germany was "the Third Reich."

Reichsluftfahrtministerium (RLM): German Air Ministry; Goering's headquarters, it controlled all aspects of German aviation.

Reichsverteidigung (RVT): the organization responsible for the air defense of Germany.

Rotte: tactical element of two aircraft.

Rottenflieger: wingman; the second man in a Rotte.

Rottenfuehrer: leader of an element of two aircraft.

Schlageter: JG 26's honor title; commemorated Albert Leo Schlageter.

Schnellkampfgeschwader (SKG): fast bomber wing (contained Bf 110, Bf 109, or FW 190 fighter-bombers).

Schwarm: flight of four aircraft (pl. **Schwaerme**); all German fighter formations were made up of units of Schwaerme.

Schwarmfuehrer: flight leader.

Sitzkrieg: "sitting war"—the "phony war" in western Europe between September 1939 and April 1940.

Stab: staff.

Stabskette: staff flight of three aircraft.

Stabsschwarm: staff flight of four aircraft.

Staffel (St): squadron (pl. **Staffeln**).

Staffelfuehrer: squadron leader (temporary or probationary).

Staffelkapitaen: squadron leader—usually a Leutnant, Oberleutnant, or Hauptmann.

Staffelhund: "squadron dog"—a unit mascot.

Wehrmacht: armed forces—the German Armed Forces is implied.

Werkenummer (W.Nr.): aircraft serial number.

Winkel: chevron.

English Abreviations

KIA: killed in action.

KIFA: killed in a flying accident.

POW: prisoner of war.

RAF: Royal Air Force.

RCAF: Royal Canadian Air Force.

RNAF: Royal Norwegian Air Force.

USAAF: US Army Air Force.

Index

Abbeville-Drucat, 23, 35, 37, 57, 66, 72, 73, 74, 75, 76, 77, 79, 80, 99
Adamsonstaffel, 10, 16, 84, 93, 108, 111
Adolph, Hptm. Walter, 49
Ahrens, Uffz. Erich, 144
Ain el Gazala, Libya, 45-46
Andel, Lt. Peter, 145
Anselment, Gefr. Reinhard, 146
Arado Ar 68, 7
Audembert, 27, 29, 31, 32, 37, 55, 60, 67, 69, 100, 101

Babenz, Obfw. Emil, 107
Backeberg, Uffz. Heinz, 116
Backhaus, Uffz. Hans, 70
Bartels, Oblt. Werner, 24, 159
Battmer, Fliegerstabsingenieur Ernst, 68, 161
Bauerhenne, Fw. F. W., 23
Beauvais, 114
Beese, Oblt. Artur, 13, 27, 106
Berg, Maj. Ernst Freiherr von, 12, 17
Beyer, Oblt. Georg, 26, 158
Bierwirth, Obfw. Heinz, 79
Bissel, 152
Blotko, Flg. Guenter, 18
Blume, Lt. Walter, 18
Bock, Uffz. Heinz, 30, 65
Boenninghardt, 7
Boehm-Tettelbach, Oblt. Karl, 9
Borris, Maj. Karl, 82, 86, 106, 138, 161
Boissy-le-Bois, 136, 137, 138
Bracher, Oblt. Fritz, 139
Braun, Uffz. Ernst, 65
Braun, Fw. Walter, 65, 159
Bremer, Uffz. Herbert, 71
Brest-Guipavas, 50
Buchmann, Gefr. Matthias, 39, 45
Buerschgens, Lt. Josef, 12, 25, 26

Caffiers, 22, 25, 27, 28, 29, 33, 34, 98
Calais, 15, 22
Cambrai, 102, 113, 116, 117
Cazaux, 86
Celle, 104, 154
Chievres, 19
Christinnecke, Lt. Hans, 26
Cologne-Ostheim, 6, 7, 8, 9, 97
Cognac, France, 64
Coquelles, 85
Crump, Oblt. Peter, 66, 78, 116, 117, 118, 119, 146, 149

Diepholz, 15
Dietze, Lt. Gottfried, 144, 145
Dinort, Hptm. Oskar, 6, 97, 156
Dippel, Lt. Hans-Georg, 127, 128
Dortmund, 13
Duesseldorf, 6, 7, 9, 97

Ebbighausen, Hptm. Karl, 21, 31, 157, 158
Ebeling, Oblt. Heinz, 25, 159
Ebersberger, Oblt. Kurt, 74, 76, 109
Eberz, Fw. Bernhard, 19
Eder, Maj. George-Peter, 142
Edmann, Obfw. Johann, 84, 107
Ellenrieder, Obfw. Xaver, 122
Epinoy, 113
Erpenbach, Uffz. Paul, 108

Fischer, Uffz. Oswald, 65, 67, 100, 112
Flensburg, 104, 155
Focke-Wulf FW 190, 50, 65, 66, 92, 96, 133, 148
Frantz, Fhr. Ulrich, 133
Freuwoerth , Obfw. Wilhelm, 116
Friesoythe, Germany, 153
Fritsch, Lt. Paul, 116
Fritsch, Uffz. Artur, 144
Fronhoefer, Fw. Willy, 29
Fuerstenau, 132, 146

Gaertner, Obfw. Josef, 65
Gaeth, Hptm. Wilhelm, 67, 161
Galland, Genlt. Adolf, 15, 22, 25, 26, 29, 30, 32, 37, 60, 61, 66, 99, 103, 140, 141, 145, 158, 159, 160, 161, 162

Galland, Lt. Paul, 66
Galland, Hptm. Wilhelm-Ferdinand "Wutz," 35, 66, 77, 78, 111, 112
Geburtig, Oblt. Hans, 84
Gehrke, Uffz. Heinz, 103, 104, 162
Geisshardt, Hptm. Fritz, 121, 124
Gela, Sicily, 40, 41, 42, 43, 44, 99
Glunz, Oblt. Adolf "Addi," 76, 77, 102, 114, 115, 116, 135, 162
Goerbig, Obfw. Kurt, 60
Goering, Reichsmarschall Herman, 22, 23, 60, 62, 93
Goetz, Maj. Franz, 104, 148, 151, 163
Gomann, Uffz. Heinz, 119
Grabmann, Hptm. Walter, 8
Grad, Uffz. Hermann, 137, 146
Gruenlinger, Fw. Walter, 81, 82, 161
Grzymalla, Obfw. Gerhard, 65
Guenther, Obfw. Alfred, 118
Guhl, Lt. Hermann, 134
Guyancourt, 131,133, 134, 135, 138

Hackl, Maj. Anton, 151, 152
Hagedorn, Ogfr., 29
Hager, Fw. Robert, 84, 86
Haiboeck, Oblt. Josef, 29
Halbmass, Hptfw., 41
Handrick, Maj. Gotthardt, 16, 22, 24, 158
Hasselmann, Oblt., 18, 22, 24
Heckmann, Oblt. Fred, 141, 142
Hegenauer, Lt. Bruno, 36, 69
Heitmann, Obfw. Hans, 84
Henrici, Oblt. Eberhard, 15, 27, 157
Herzog, Fw. Gerhard, 65
Hesepe, 143, 144
Hilgendorff, Oblt. Viktor, 101, 161, 162
Hoernig, Oblt. Franz, 27, 157
Hoffmann, Uffz. Johannes, 154
Hofmann, Oblt. Wilhelm, 144, 152
Holtey, Oblt. Hubertus Freiherr von, 63
Holtz, Ogfr. Norbert, 107, 108, 111
Holzapfel, Gefr. Peter,, 159
Hoppe, Oblt. Helmut, 113
Horch, Uffz. Otto, 142
Horten, Oblt. Walter, 19, 23, 30
Humburg, Obfw. Heinrich, 29, 122

Jaeckel, Obfw. Konrad, 65
Jaros, Obfw. Otto, 65
Jauer, Fw. Erich, 83
JG 2, 49, 50, 65
JG 26, 7, 42, 66
Johannsen, Lt. Hans, 41, 42, 47
Juris, Ogfr., 44
Jutrzenka, Uffz. Konrad von, 65

Kalitzki, Obfw. Willi, 84
Kehl, Lt. Dietrich, 113
Kelch, Hptm. Guenther, 82, 83, 88, 89
Kemethmueller, Lt. Heinz, 83, 138
Kempf, Lt. Karl-Heinz, 129, 141
Kestel, Fw. Melchior, 89
Kiefner, Lt. Georg, 136, 141
Kienitz, Hptm. Walter, 97, 157
Klar, Fw. Martin, 65
Kleffner, Uffz. Erich, 116
Kleinecke, Gefr. Robert, 53
Knueppel, Oblt. Herwig, 158
Kosse, Oblt., Wolfgang, 50
Kothe, Fw., 22, 29
Kraft, Fw. Werner, 90
Kranefeld, Oblt. Kurt, 86, 107
Kraus, Oblt. Theobald, 134
Krieg, Uffz. Heinrich, 116, 119
Krug, Oblt. Hans, 158
Krupinski, Hptm. Walter, 145
Kuehn, Fw., 6
Kuepper, Fw. Arnold, 65
Kukla, Uffz. Hans, 146

Lang, Hptm. Emil, 142, 146, 161
Langhammer, Gefr., 22, 29
Latka, Fw. Wilhelm , 84
Laub, Obfw. Karl, 146
Laube, Obfw. Ernst, 43, 47
Le Perray, 142

Lenz, Oblt. Harald, 134
Leppla, Lt., 9
Les Mesnuls, 140
Leykauf, Oblt. Erwin, 122
Liebeck, Uffz. Horst, 65
Liegescourt, 53
Lille-Nord, 95, 126, 127, 128, 129, 130
Lille-Vendeville, 92, 93, 95, 96, 105, 107, 122
Lindemann, Oblt. Theo, 47
Losigkeit, Oblt. Fritz, 12, 17, 18, 33, 157
Lueders, Obfw. Franz, 11, 65

Maeder, Flg., 29
Malm, Uffz. Willibald, 154
Marquise, 30, 34
Martin, Obfw. Max, 52, 84
Matoni, Hptm. Walter, 117, 134
Mayer, Hptm. Egon, 74
Meihs, Uffz. Heinz, 144
Melsbroek, 102, 143
Menge, Lt. Robert, 51, 108, 110
Messerschmitt Bf 108, 73
Messerschmitt Bf 109, 7, 15, 22, 23, 31, 34, 38, 49, 60, 66, 92, 133
Meyer, Fw. Hermann, 113
Meyer, Uffz. Albert, 30, 32, 116
Meyer, Obfw. Walter, 121
Mietusch, Maj. Klaus, 42, 47, 82, 83, 84, 92, 103, 125, 126, 130, 134, 135, 145, 161, 162
Mischkot, Lt. Bruno, 144
Mondry, Uffz. Georg, 41, 45, 47
Moorsele, Belgium, 57, 59, 66, 86, 88, 89, 90, 91, 101
Muehlheim-Essen, 12, 13, 15, 16
Mueller-Duehe, Lt. Gerhard, 24, 26
Muencheberg, Hptm. Joachim, 19, 22, 25, 26, 27, 28, 38, 39, 40, 41, 42, 47, 63, 66, 73, 74, 99, 160

Naumann, Hptm. Johannes "Hans," 19, 53, 112, 118, 120, 146, 161
Neu, Oblt. Wolfgang, 108, 109
Nibel, Lt. Theo, 146, 149
Niese, Uffz. Alfred, 89
Nordhorn-Clausheide, 133, 149, 150, 152

Odendorf, 7
Oemler, Uffz. Gerhard, 53
Oerlinghausen, 11
Olemotz, Gefr., 23

Patzke, Uffz. Guenther, 83
Pautner, Uffz. Robert, 125
Perez, Uffz. Horst, 31, 33, 65
Philipp, Hptm. Gerhard, 161
Pingel, Hptm. Rolf, 35, 36, 100
Pomaska, Oblt. Alfred, 158
Plantluenne, 133, 145, 151
Priller, Obst. Josef "Pips," 54, 59, 80, 81, 82, 83, 84, 92, 93, 94, 95, 101, 104, 105, 107, 112, 115, 120, 129, 131, 132, 134, 141, 149, 151, 155, 161, 162
Pritze, Uffz. Hans, 83
Puschenjack, Ogfr. Otto, 144

Radener, Lt. Waldemar, 76, 152
Ramthun, Lt. Friedrich, 141
Reinsehlen, 103, 147
Reischer, Oblt. Peter, 134
Rose, Ofhr. Wolfgang, 110
Rothenberg, Oblt., 30
Rotterdam-Waalhaven, 62
Royal Air Force
No. 54 Sqd., 24
No. 56 Sqd., 146
No. 88 Sqd., 120
No. 92 Sqd., 51
No. 222 Sqd., 75
No. 245 Sqd., 155
No. 331 Sqd., 114
No. 443 Sqd., 135
Ruestenkamp, Uffz., 109
Ruppert, Oblt. Kurt, 49, 52, 53, 82, 88, 89, 90

Rysavy, Lt. Martin, 14

Sattler, Uffz. Ludwig, 146
Schammert, Uffz., 65
Schauder, Oblt. Paul, 134
Schiffbauer, Obfw. Robert, 65
Schild, Lt. Heinrich "Jan," 71, 154
Schleich, Obst. Eduard Ritter von, 7, 10
Schleswig, Germany, 155
Schmid, Hptm. Johann, 58
Schmidt, Lt. Gottfried "Cognac," 85, 134
Schmidtke, Fw. Kurt, 107, 108, 109
Schneider, Oblt. Walter, 30, 57, 101
Schneider, Uffz. Friedrich, 51, 52, 55, 61
Schoehl , Uffz. Horst-Guenther, 107, 108
Schoepfel, Maj. Gerhard, 26, 28, 29, 47, 50, 53, 67, 68, 69, 92, 98, 158, 159
Schroedter, Hptm. Rolf, 26
Schroepfer, Uffz. Martin, 65
Schulwitz, Lt. Gerhard "Bubi," 144, 152
Schwan, Uffz. Werner, 141
Schwarz, Fw. Erich, 108
Seifert, Maj. Johannes, 69, 92, 157
Siebert, Uffz., 29, 44
Sieling, Oblt. Wilfried, 67, 69, 161
Sinz, Fw. Hermann, 154
Soeffing, Lt. Waldemar, 72, 146
Sprick, Oblt. Gustav "Micky," 23, 26, 31, 55, 98, 160
St. Brieuc, Brittany, 52, 99
St. Omer, 68, 70, 73
St. Omer-Arques, 59, 70
St. Omer-Clairmarais, 54, 55, 56
St. Omer-Ft. Rouge, 71
St. Omer-Wizernes, 66, 105
Staiger, Hptm. Hermann, 127, 135
Stammberger, Lt. Otto "Stotto," 53, 87, 88, 89, 102, 113, 114
Steindl, Hptm. Peter-Paul, 124
Sternberg, Lt. Horst, 58, 59
Stevede-Coesfeld, 144, 145
Stoeckl, Gefr., 29
Straub, Fw. Karl, 65,1 58
Stumpf, Uffz. Walter, 144, 145
Supermarine Spitfire, 22, 50, 66

Thuilot, Fw. Paul, 86
Tippe, Uffz. Erhard, 135
Todt, Lt. Ernst, 125

Ungar, Fw. Friedrich, 143, 151
Unger, Lt., 9
US Army Air Forces
2nd Air Division, 148
4th Fighter Group, 58
55th Fighter Group, 69, 129
56th Fighter Group, 111
92nd Bomb Group, 87
306th Bomber Group, 112
353rd Fighter Group, 125
361st Fighter Group, 107, 125, 137
359th Fighter Group, 142
492nd Bomb Group, 134

Varrelbusch, Germany, 146, 151
Villacoublay, 15, 103, 134, 139
Vitry-en-Artois, 102, 113, 114, 116, 117, 118, 119
Voelmle, Lt. Dieter, 134
Vogt, Oblt. Gerhard, 57, 138, 150, 152

Waelter, Uffz. Heinrich, 84
Weber, Fw. Otto, 151
Weiss, Uffz. Franz, 146
Werl, 15
Wendt, Oblt. Kuno, 16
Wevelghem, Belgium, 58, 59, 60, 66, 80-86, 101, 107, 108, 109, 110, 111, 123, 124
Wilde, Hptm., 22
Willius, Fw. Karl, 107
Witt, Maj. Hans-Hugo, 7, 16, 17, 98, 158
Wodarczyk, Ogfr. Heinz, 111, 131, 134
Woege, Uffz., 83

Zech, Obfw. Werner, 151